The Sociologist and the Historian

The Sociologist and the Historian

Pierre Bourdieu
and Roger Chartier

Translated by David Fernbach

polity

First published in French as *Le Sociologue et l'historien* © Éditions Agone, Marseille, & Raisons d'Agir, Paris, France, 2010

This English edition © Polity Press, 2015

Polity Press
65 Bridge Street
Cambridge CB2 1UR, UK

Polity Press
350 Main Street
Malden, MA 02148, USA

ISBN-13: 978-0-7456-7958-7
ISBN-13: 978-0-7456-7959-4 (pb)

A catalogue record for this book is available from the British Library.

Library of Congress Cataloging-in-Publication Data

Bourdieu, Pierre, 1930-2002
  [Le sociologue et l'historien. English]
  The sociologist and the historian / Pierre Bourdieu, Roger Chartier.
    pages cm
  Translation of the author's Le sociologue et l'historien.
  ISBN 978-0-7456-7958-7 (hardback) – ISBN 0-7456-7958-7 (hardcover) – ISBN 978-0-7456-7959-4 (paperback) – ISBN 0-7456-7959-5 (paperback) 1. Bourdieu, Pierre, 1903-2002–Interviews. 2. Chartier, Roger, 1945—Interviews. 3. Sociologists–France–Interviews.
  4. Historians–France–Interviews. I. Chartier, Roger, 1945- II. Title.
  HM479.B68A513 2015
  301.0944–dc23
                        2014039887

Typeset in 11 on 14 pt Sabon
by Toppan Best-set Premedia Limited
Printed and bound in the UK by CPI Group (UK) Ltd, Croydon, CR0 4YY

For further information on Polity, visit our website: politybooks.com

Contents

v

Preface

My first impression on reading these interviews conducted with Pierre Bourdieu in 1988 was to find him
just as he had remained in my memory from these five
broadcasts: energetic, humorous, impassioned. The
merit of this little book, I believe, is that his way of
thinking can be followed particularly closely in this
lively exchange, freed from the shrouds that sometimes
cover it, whether the magisterial authority conferred by
his chair at the Collège de France[1] or the polemical
debates of the sociologist deeply engaged in his era.
Without obscuring the continuity and coherence of a
work based from its beginnings on the same categories
of analysis and the same demand for critical clarity,
these five interviews introduce us to a rather different

---

[1] Bourdieu delivered his inaugural lecture as professor of sociology at the Collège de France on 23 April 1982. It was
published by Éditions de Minuit under the title *Leçon sur la
leçon* ['Lecture on the Lecture', in *In Other Words: Essays
Towards a Reflexive Sociology* (Cambridge: Polity, 1990)].

Bourdieu, less imprisoned by the roles that he subsequently chose, or that were imposed on him. A Bourdieu joyful, vivacious, ironic with others but also with himself; a Bourdieu confident about the scientific breaks that his work effected, but also ever ready for dialogue with other disciplines and other approaches.

These conversations should not be read without recalling the difference in time; rather, their specific date should be borne in mind. In 1987, France Culture, of which Jean-Marie Borzeix[2] was then director, wanted to include Bourdieu in its series *À voix nue* ('With Bare Voice'). If the choice of his interlocutor fell on a historian who was neither a beginner nor one of the most visible, this was certainly because the admiration and intellectual friendship that I felt for Bourdieu had already been expressed by his presence on several of the programmes I produced – and still produce – one Monday a month for *Les lundis de l'histoire*.[3] One programme, devoted to his two books that appeared within a short timespan – *La Distinction* and *Le Sens pratique*[4] – had him in dialogue with Patrick Fridenson

---

[2] Jean-Marie Borzeix ran the radio channel France Culture from 1984 to 1997.

[3] On 24 October 1983, for example, in a programme devoted to the history and sociology of art, with Carlo Ginzburg and Louis Marin, and on 8 July 1985 on the subject of Alain Viala's book *Naissance de l'écrivain: Sociologie de la littérature à l'âge classique*, with Christian Jouhaud and Alain Viala.

[4] Published by Éditions de Minuit in 1979 and 1980 respectively. [*Distinction: A Social Critique of the Judgement of Taste* (Cambridge, MA: Harvard University Press, 1984); *The Logic of Practice* (Cambridge: Polity, 1990).]

and Georges Duby, with whom he enjoyed a bond of mutual esteem.[5] This remains for me one of the strongest memories of these broadcasts. At a time when *Distinction* had been the target of fierce attacks from certain historians, who either could not understand it or did so all too well, this exchange showed, conversely, that both historian and sociologist had to understand struggles over classification as being just as real as class struggles (if indeed they could be separated from one another), and that conflicting representations of the social world produced it at the same time as they expressed it.

The Bourdieu of 1987 was for many people the author of *Distinction*. Polemic and media attention to this book had brought the sociologist to the front of the intellectual and public stage.[6] But before the publication of *Distinction*, Bourdieu already had a long past as a researcher and a strong and substantial body of work,[7] marked by his ethnological

---

[5] This programme in the *Lundis de l'histoire* series was broadcast on 25 February 1980.

[6] Bourdieu had presented his book on television in the course of a programme in the *Apostrophes* series, where he was the guest of Bernard Pivot along with Fernand Braudel and Max Gallo, on 21 December 1979. The programme title was 'The Historian, the Sociologist and the Novelist'.

[7] We can take the measure of this thanks to the very remarkable work of Yvette Delsaut and Marie-Christine Rivière, *Bibliographie des travaux de Pierre Bourdieu, suivi d'un entretien sur l'esprit de la recherche* (Paris: Le Temps des cerises, 2002; new edition 2009).

---

publications on Kabylia,[8] his analyses of the French educational system,[9] his collective investigations of the social uses of photography[10] and of museum visiting,[11]

---

[8] Pierre Bourdieu, *Esquisse d'une théorie de la pratique, précédé de trois études d'ethnologie kabyle* (Geneva: Droz, 1972) [*Outline of a Theory of Practice* (Cambridge: Cambridge University Press, 1977)].

[9] Pierre Bourdieu and Jean-Claude Passeron, *Les Héritiers: Les étudiants et la culture* (Paris: Minuit, 1964) [*The Inheritors: French Students and their Relation to Culture* (Chicago: University of Illinois Press, 1979)]; Pierre Bourdieu and Jean-Claude Passeron, *La Reproduction: Éléments pour une théorie du système d'enseignement* (Paris: Minuit, 1970) [*Reproduction in Education, Society and Culture* (London: Sage, 1977)]; Pierre Bourdieu and Monique de Saint-Martin, 'Les catégories de l'entendement professoral' ['The Categories of Professorial Judgment', in *Homo Academicus* (Cambridge: Polity, 1988), pp. 194–225], and 'Épreuve scolaire et consécration sociale: Les classes préparatoires aux grandes écoles', *Actes de la recherche en sciences sociales*, May 1975, no. 3, pp. 68–93, and September 1981, no. 39, pp. 3–70. The latter two studies are mentioned by Bourdieu in the course of the discussions that follow.

[10] Luc Boltanski, Pierre Bourdieu, Robert Castel and Jean-Claude Chamboredon, *Un art moyen: Essai sur les usages sociaux de la photographie* (Paris: Minuit, 1965) [*Photography: The Social Uses of an Ordinary Art* (Cambridge: Polity, 1989)].

[11] Pierre Bourdieu, André Darbel and Dominique Schnapper, *L'Amour de l'art: Les musées et leur public* (Paris: Minuit, 1966) [*The Love of Art: European Art Museums and their Public* (Cambridge: Polity, 1990)].

---

and his theoretical reflections on the logics of practice. These main lines in no way exhaust the astounding vitality of a research that was always open to new topics, and that also focused on such varied objects as opinion polls,[12] matrimonial strategies,[13] haute couture,[14] the practices of sports,[15] and the sociology

---

[12] Pierre Bourdieu, 'L'opinion publique n'existe pas', *Noroît*, February 1971, no. 155 ['Public Opinion Does Not Exist', in Armand Mattelart and Seth Siegelaub (eds.), *Communication and Class Struggle* (New York: International General, 1979), pp. 124–30].

[13] Pierre Bourdieu, 'Les stratégies matrimoniales dans les systèmes de reproduction', *Annales ESC*, July–October 1972, pp. 1105–27 ['Marriage Strategies as Strategies of Social Reproduction', in Robert Forster and Orest Ranum (eds.), *Family and Society* (Baltimore: Johns Hopkins University Press, 1976), pp. 117–44] and 'De la règle aux stratégies: Entretien avec Pierre Lamaison', *Terrains*, March 1985, pp. 93–100 ['From Rules to Strategies', *Cultural Anthropology*, 1986, no. 1, pp. 110–20].

[14] Pierre Bourdieu, 'Haute couture et haute culture', *Noroît*, November 1974, no. 192, and with Yvette Delsaut, 'Le couturier et sa griffe: Contribution à une théorie de la magie', *Actes de la recherche en sciences sociales*, January 1975, no. 1, pp. 7–36.

[15] Pierre Bourdieu, 'Pratiques sportives et pratiques sociales', in *Actes du VIIe Congrès international de l'HISPA*, INSEP, 1978, vol. 1, pp. 17–37 ['Sport and Social Class', *Social Science Information*, 1978, no. 6, pp. 810–40].

of employers[16] and of French bishops.[17] A number of these analyses, often presented in the form of interviews or lectures, were brought together in a short volume, *Questions de sociologie*.[18] In the 1980s, three books were milestones in Bourdieu's intellectual development as a sociologist after he had been appointed professor at the Collège de France: in 1982, *Ce que parler veut dire*;[19] in 1984, what was undoubtedly the most difficult book for him, *Homo Academicus*;[20]

---

[16] Pierre Bourdieu and Monique de Saint Martin, 'Le patronat', *Actes de la recherche en sciences sociales*, March–April 1978, no. 20–1, pp. 3–82.

[17] Pierre Bourdieu and Monique de Saint Martin, 'La sainte famille: L'épiscopat français dans le champ du pouvoir', *Actes de la recherche en sciences sociales*, November 1982, no. 44–5, pp. 2–53.

[18] Pierre Bourdieu, *Questions de sociologie* (Paris: Minuit, 1980) [*Sociology in Question* (London: Sage, 1993)].

[19] Pierre Bourdieu, *Ce que parler veut dire: L'économie des échanges linguistiques* (Paris: Fayard, 1982) [*Language and Symbolic Power* (Cambridge: Polity, 1991)]. This book was the occasion for a second appearance on *Apostrophes* on 20 October 1982, along with Jacques Cellard, Auguste Lebreton, Joël Houssin and Pierre Perret, in a programme under the title 'En jacter des vertes et des pas mûres'.

[20] Pierre Bourdieu, *Homo Academicus* (Paris: Minuit, 1984) [*Homo Academicus* (Cambridge: Polity, 1988)]. It was in connection with this book, and still more so with his report for the Collège de France, *Neuf propositions pour l'enseignement de l'avenir* ['Proposals for the Future of Education', in *Political Interventions* (London: Verso, 2008, pp. 156–9], that Bourdieu appeared for a third time on *Apostrophes*, in a broadcast entitled 'De l'école à l'université', along with Jean-Pierre Chevènement, Henri Tézenas and Paul Guth.

and, a few months before our exchanges, a collection of pieces delivered orally, *Choses dites*.[21]

The Bourdieu of *À voix nue* was preparing *Les Règles de l'art*,[22] as shown by the passionate way in which he mentions his work in progress on Manet and Flaubert. A number of essays published in English had accompanied his reflections on the specific characteristics of the intellectual and artistic fields,[23] as had also the lectures he gave at Princeton in 1986 in the series 'Christian Gauss Seminars in Criticism', and again, in some respects, his study of Heidegger, published in book form the same year as these interviews.[24] This is the Bourdieu we should try to listen to here, as if we were still unaware that he would later publish *La Noblesse d'État*, *Méditations pascaliennes*, *La Domination*

---

[21] Pierre Bourdieu, *Choses dites* (Paris: Minuit, 1987) [*In Other Words: Essays Towards a Reflexive Sociology*].

[22] Pierre Bourdieu, *Les Règles de l'art: Genèse et structure du champ littéraire* (Paris: Éditions du Seuil, 1992) [*The Rules of Art: Genesis and Structure of the Literary Field* [Cambridge: Polity, 1996)].

[23] Pierre Bourdieu, 'The Field of Cultural Production, or the Economic World Reversed', *Poetics*, 1983, vol. 12, no. 4–5, pp. 311–56, and 'The Historical Genesis of a Pure Aesthetic', *Journal of Aesthetics and Art Criticism*, 1987, vol. 46, special issue, pp. 201–10. These two texts and eight others are reprinted in Pierre Bourdieu, *The Field of Cultural Production: Essays on Art and Literature* (Cambridge: Polity, 1993).

[24] Pierre Bourdieu, 'L'ontologie politique de Martin Heidegger', *Actes de la recherche en sciences sociales*, November 1975, no. 5–6, pp. 109–56; *L'Ontologie politique de Martin Heidegger* (Paris: Minuit, 1988) [*The Political Ontology of Martin Heidegger* (Cambridge: Polity, 1996)].

---

masculine and *Les Structures sociales de l'économie*,[25] not to mention the more directly political texts published by Raisons d'agir.[26]

On the historians' side, three facts must be recalled to understand certain themes in our conversations of 1988. First of all, history was still the most public and most visible discipline out of all the social sciences, not only thanks to the books of its masters, which sometimes became bestsellers, but also with the success of great multi-volume undertakings that French publishers did not shy away from and that found both buyers and translators. For example, the five-volume *Histoire de la vie privée* edited by Philippe Ariès and Georges Duby, which was published by Éditions du Seuil between 1985 and 1987, and, on a more modest scale, the *Histoire de l'édition française* that I was pleased to edit together with Henri-Jean Martin, the four volumes

---

[25] Pierre Bourdieu, *La Noblesse d'État: Grandes écoles et esprit de corps* (Paris: Minuit, 1989) [*The State Nobility: Elite Schools in the Field of Power* (Cambridge: Polity, 1996)]; *Méditations pascaliennes* (Paris: Seuil, 1997) [*Pascalian Meditations* (Cambridge: Polity, 1999)]; *La Domination masculine* (Paris: Seuil, 1998) [*Masculine Domination* (Cambridge: Polity, 2001)]; *Les Structures sociales de l'économie* (Paris: Seuil, 2000) [*The Social Structures of the Economy* (Cambridge: Polity, 2003)].

[26] For this publishing house launched in 1996 with his *Sur la television* [*On Television* (Cambridge: Polity, 2011)] Bourdieu went on to produce *Contre-feux* (1998) [*Counterfire: Against the Tyranny of the Market* (London: Verso, 2003)] and *Contre-feux 2: Pour un mouvement social européen* (2001) [*Firing Back: Against the Tyranny of the Market 2* (London: Verso, 2003)].

---

of which were published by Promodis between 1982 and 1986.

On the other hand, French historians had by then begun to distance themselves from the principles of analysis that had founded the domination – or at least the intellectual domination – of *Annales*, visible in a preference for massive sources, a quantitative treatment of those sources, and the creation of series. Challenged from outside, for example, by the propositions of Italian micro-history, but also from within the *Annales* tradition itself, this model of intelligibility had broken up in favour of other approaches, which privileged collective representations more than objective classifications, singular appropriations more than statistical distributions, conscious strategies more than unconscious determinations. Hence the debates, no doubt rather futile for Bourdieu, between the former primacy given to series and structures, and the more recent attention given to actors, or regarding the distances or affinities between the categories deployed by the historian and the language of historical actors themselves.

Finally, though still only timidly, history had begun to question itself. Far removed from Bourdieu's ways of thinking, some major texts by Paul Veyne, Michel de Certeau and Paul Ricoeur[27] had indicated the tension that existed between the discipline's intention of seeking knowledge and the necessarily narrative form of its

---

[27] Paul Veyne, *Comment on écrit l'histoire: Essai d'épistémologie* (Paris: Seuil, 1971); Michel de Certeau, *L'Écriture de l'histoire* (Paris: Gallimard, 1975); Paul Ricoeur, *Temps et récit*, 3 vols. (Paris: Seuil, 1983–5).

---

writing. For some historians, if not for the profession as a whole, this presented a further reason for the collapse of inherited certainties and a strong incitement to reflect not only on the scientific nature of their discipline, but also, and conversely, on the cognitive capacity of fiction, as Bourdieu was doing in his study of Flaubert.[28]

These interviews accordingly make it possible to locate a moment in Bourdieu's relationship with history and historians. His criticism was sharp, reproaching them for unduly universalizing their categories of analysis and insufficiently questioning the social and historical construction of partitions and classifications that they too often took as natural objects. At the same time, however, Bourdieu respected the work of certain historians, French and foreign, who found a generous welcome in the pages of *Actes de la recherche en sciences sociales*,[29] or were published in the collection *Le*

---

[28] It was in this perspective that my work on Molière's *George Dandin* was located, as mentioned in the following interviews and published as 'George Dandin, ou le social en représentation', *Annales: Histoire, sciences sociales*, March–April 1994, pp. 277–309 ['From Court Festivity to City Spectators', in Roger Chartier, *Forms and Meanings: Texts, Performances, and Audiences from Codex to Computer* (Philadelphia: University of Pennsylvania Press, 1995, pp. 43–82)].

[29] Before 1988, for example, these foreign historians included the art historians Svetlana Alpers, Michael Baxandall, Francis Haskell, Dario Gamboni and Enrico Castelnuovo, as well as Carlo Ginzburg, Edward Thompson, Eric Hobsbawm, Robert Darnton, Carl Schorske and David Sabean, while French historians included Maurice Agulhon, Christophe Charle, Dominique Julia, Lucette Le Van-Lemesle and Gérard Noiriel.

---

sens commun that he edited for Éditions de Minuit.[30] Shortly before our interviews, I had myself published an article in *Actes*,[31] and had two conversations with Bourdieu on the subject of reading and cultural history.[32]

---

[30] For example, Erwin Panofsky, *Architecture gothique et pensée scolastique*, preceded by *L'Abbé Suger à Saint-Denis*, translated with a preface by Pierre Bourdieu, 1967; François Furet and Jacques Ozouf, *Lire et écrire: L'alphabétisation des français de Calvin à Jules Ferry*, 1977; François de Dainville, *L'Éducation des Jésuites (XVIe–XVIIIe siècles)*, texts edited and introduced by Marie-Madeleine Compère, 1978; and Alain Viala, *Naissance de l'écrivain: Sociologie de la littérature à l'âge classique*, 1985, to which should be added two books that, despite not being by historians, still had a key importance for this discipline: Richard Hoggart's *The Uses of Literacy*, published in French as *La culture du pauvre: Étude sur le style de vie des classes populaires en Angleterre*, with an introduction by Jean-Claude Passeron in 1970, and Jack Goody, *The Domestication of the Savage Mind*, published in French as *La Raison graphique: Le domestication de la pensée sauvage*, translated and introduced by Jean Bazin and Alban Bensa in 1978.

[31] Roger Chartier, 'Science sociale et découpage régional: Note sur deux débats (1820–1920)', *Actes de la recherche en sciences sociales*, November 1980, no. 35, pp. 27–36.

[32] Pierre Bourdieu and Roger Chartier, 'La lecture: Une pratique culturelle', in Roger Chartier (ed.), *Pratiques de la lecture* (Paris: Rivages, 1985), pp. 217–39. (This dialogue took place on 18 September 1982 at the Collège d'échanges contemporains de Saint-Maximin and was broadcast on the France Culture programme 'Dialogues' on 7 December 1982.) Also Pierre Bourdieu, Roger Chartier and Robert Darnton, 'Dialogue à propos de l'histoire culturelle', *Actes de la recherche en sciences sociales*, September 1985, no. 59, pp. 86–93.

The violence of polemics that were ever more bitter, the return to a primacy of politics and the individual that some people proclaimed at the time of the controversies aroused by the bicentennial of the French Revolution, as well as the vogue for national history, led Bourdieu to a more forceful critique of history and historians, as shown in his 1995 interview with the German historian Lutz Raphael.[33] His tone is no longer that of 1988, and his indictment, in which only a few names are spared, is remorseless: history (at least French history) is denounced here en bloc, for its rejection of any critical reflexivity, its taste for false oppositions, its attraction to bad philosophy, its ignorance of the classic works of the social sciences, and the preference it gives to futile epistemological discussions at the expense of research practices that are in fact the genuine site of theoretical reflection. This pitiless judgement, whether it is seen as well founded or unjust, well targeted or too indistinct, had shifted quite a bit from the critical but friendly tone of the 1988 exchanges. This is why I am happy to be able to rediscover this precious moment of a dialogue damaged for a while by injuries and misunderstandings, but subsequently renewed. Several conversations with Bourdieu in *Les lundis de l'histoire* remain shining memories for me, inspired, as ten years previously, by the warmth of a discussion that was demanding but peaceable: for example, an interview about *Méditations pascaliennes* inspired by the memory

---

[33] Pierre Bourdieu, 'Sur les rapports entre la sociologie et l'histoire en Allemagne et en France: Entretien avec Lutz Raphael', *Actes de la recherche en sciences sociales*, March 1995, no. 106–7, pp. 108–22.

of Louis Marin, who had been Bourdieu's friend since their years at the École normale supérieure,[34] or, on *La Domination masculine*, a dialogue with Arlette Farge on the marvellous mystery that sometimes breaks the iron laws of the social world and makes possible the enchantment of unexpected encounters.[35]

The lightness of tone that marks these five conversations should not, however, lead us to forget that they are also marked by Bourdieu's evident anxiety in his efforts to understand the violent resistance to his analyses – not only on the part of his opponents – and the tensions characteristic of a work on social spaces, whether the world of the university or society as a whole, in which the sociologist himself participates – 'as a native', as Bourdieu puts it. Hence, for him, the difficult but indispensable task of a discipline that, by dissolving reassuring misunderstandings, makes possible a more lucid comprehension of the mechanisms that govern dominations and subjections, but at the price of disillusion. 'The sociologist is insufferable', he maintains, and not only to others, but also to himself, as he finds himself situated within the social field that he is analysing. We discover in Bourdieu's words the painful 'schizophrenia' (a word he uses) that results from this position, no doubt unique in the social sciences, in which the subject who produces knowledge is at the same time part of the object to be known.

---

[34] *Les lundis de l'histoire*, programme broadcast 12 May 1997.
[35] *Les lundis de l'histoire*, programme broadcast 19 October 1998.

Difficult to live and to assume, this division of oneself that sociological work implies also lies at the bottom of the 'rational utopianism' that founds it. In fact, it is only by displaying the determinisms that constrain the actors of the social world (including the sociologist) that a way is opened for the critique of illusory appearances and deceptively self-evident phenomena, the loosening of constraints and the possibility given to each person, even if not all are able to seize it, to 'become the subject of their own thoughts'. On condition of not getting bogged down in false oppositions (for example, between individual and society, between consensus and conflict, between the objectivity of structures and the subjectivity of actors), the work of the sociologist offers mechanisms of self-defence against what the natural order of things – and of dominations – seems inexorably to impose.

Pierre Bourdieu was haunted by his responsibility. This sentiment explains his commitments, but also his torments, and – as may be read in these interviews, which restore his passionate speech as closely as possible – his trust in knowledge as alone capable of making the world, as it is, less ineluctable and less of a source of despair.

Roger Chartier
Paris, 24 November 2009

The following texts stem from five radio programmes in the series *À voix nue*, recorded on 7 and 8 December 1987 and broadcast on France Culture between 1 and 5 February 1988. Marie-Andrée Armynot du Châtelet helped with their production. They were repeated on the same channel between 28 January and 1 February 2002, following the death of Pierre Bourdieu on 23 January 2002.

I

The Sociologist's Craft

ROGER CHARTIER: It can't be easy being a sociologist, given that, when we look at the way that your work has been received, we are struck by the tremendous contradictions coming from writers' pens and existing in people's minds. Because, after all, the question is whether sociology is more fitted to mobilizing the masses or causing the labour movement to despair? How can sociological texts, which are usually illegible, be both so complex that they are impenetrable and at the same time bear a message that is particularly clear and, for some readers, radically subversive? And can sociology claim – as we sometimes get the impression – to be a dominant science, a science of sciences, while you are deconstructing it as a discipline by everything that you write? This sum of contradictions can perhaps serve as the starting point for the first of the present interviews, as they focus on a series of fundamental questions: what is sociology? What is it to be a sociologist? How should we conceive the relationship that sociology has with other disciplines which, like my own

---

discipline of history, find themselves faced with this protean and somewhat disturbing monster?

PIERRE BOURDIEU: Indeed, I do think that sociology is upsetting, but the rather obsessional feeling that I might experience as a sociologist is neutralized, despite everything, by the very contradictions between these various attacks. In particular, I think that the accusations of a political kind directed against sociology have at least the virtue of being contradictory; and in this way, they give it life. Well, it is true that sociology is not always easy to live with.

ROGER CHARTIER: Yes, since the impression is given that it is a discipline which, by its attempt at reflexivity on the social world, at the same time situates the person producing it in the very field that he is in the process of describing. In this sense, it is not easy to live with, not simply because it gives other people an image of themselves that they are often unwilling to tolerate, but also because it implicates the person producing it in the analysis itself.

PIERRE BOURDIEU: I have had the experience of such a situation: for example, when I speak about sociology to non-sociologists, non-professionals, I'm always torn between two possible strategies. The first is presenting sociology as an academic discipline, as something like history or philosophy, and in this case I get a reception that is interested but strictly academic. Or else I try to exert the specific effect of sociology, in other words try to place my listeners in a situation of self-analysis, and from that point on I know that I am exposing myself to becoming a scapegoat for the company assembled. For example, I had this experience two years ago when I went to the Brussels Philharmonic,[1] invited by an official of the Amis de la Philharmonique de Bruxelles, who, very kindly but a little naively, had asked me to come and explain my views, my representations of art, the sociology of music, and so on. And up to the last moment – I remember very well – in the car in which we were setting out in the night, I repeated to this person: 'You don't realize what you're doing, you're asking me to do something dreadful, and it will be dramatic: there will be incidents, I'll provoke insults.' He thought that I was just having the usual lecturer's stage fright. And then what I feared really did happen: it was a genuine 'happening', and for the whole of the next week this was all that people talked about in the intellectual milieu of Brussels. A friend of mine heard one of the participants say that not since the Surrealists had he heard such a heated and extraordinary debate as on that occasion. Now, the things I said were actually quite anodyne, euphemistic and neutralized. I had taken precautions. Right in front of me in the hall was an elderly lady, very well dressed, with her handbag on her knees, a bit like at the Collège de France, and I was very concerned not to shock her at all; so I was as euphemistic as possible. Despite this, however, I think that sociological 'truth'

---

[1] It has not been possible to trace the date or the subject of this Brussels lecture. Probably it paralleled the themes of 'Bourdieu attaque: Deux doigts de Ravel. Entretien avec Cyril Huvé', *Le Monde de la musique*, 6 December 1978, pp. 30–1 ['Music Lovers: Origin and Evolution of the Species', in Bourdieu, *Sociology in Question*, pp. 103–7].

– I put it in quotation marks here – is so violent that it injures people; it makes them suffer and, at the same time, people free themselves from this suffering by shifting it back to the person who is apparently causing it.

ROGER CHARTIER: That is perhaps the difference between sociology and history, which talks about dead people, and perhaps also ethnology and anthropology, which describe subjects who are only rarely, and in exceptional circumstances, confronted with discourses that speak about them.

PIERRE BOURDIEU: Indeed, here again I can answer with an example. This is a story that I find quite funny. One of my colleagues at the Collège de France, an eminent member of the Institut,[2] told me that my writings had aroused a certain resistance among members of the Institut, even outspoken resistance. And among these writings, the most shocking was an article that I published under the title 'The Categories of Professorial Understanding'[3] – parenthetically, a highly ironic title, there are very often things that make me laugh as I write them; unfortunately, there is no way of expressing laughter in writing, that's one of the big lacunas among graphic symbols. So, I gave the article this title, 'The Categories of Professorial Understanding', and in this article I analysed, on the one hand, the comments made on his students' essays by a teacher at the Lycée Fénelon who

---

[2] [The Institut de France is the learned society that includes the Académie française and other bodies. – Translator.]
[3] Bourdieu and de Saint-Martin, 'Les catégories de l'entendement professoral'.

4

taught the *khâgne*[4] class, and on the other hand the obituaries of former students of the École normale supérieure. And this eminent colleague, an Egyptologist in fact, said to me: 'All the same, you know, you did take obituaries as an object of study.' I replied: 'But my dear colleague, how can you say that to me? What is your own object if not obituaries?' And I think this gives a very good sense of the gap between sociology and history. The historian permits himself to take many things as self-evident, and even as signs of achievement. If, for example, a historian reveals hidden relationships – *liaisons*, we call them – between one particular historical character and another, he is praised and this is seen as a discovery. Whereas if I were to publish, let's say, a tenth of what would need to be said in order to understand the functioning of the world of the university – the academic fields – I would be seen as an infamous informer. On the other hand, I think that distance in time has a virtue of neutralizing – as everyone knows. In the case of sociology, however, we are always walking on hot coals, and the things we discuss are alive, they're not dead and buried.

ROGER CHARTIER: This is why we thought that this first interview could be focused on the political effects of intellectual work and, taking the case of sociology, could show how the figure of the intellectual has shifted on the French intellectual scene. By and large, from a figure that was prophetic, messianic, denunciatory, at a macroscopic level – perhaps the name of Sartre is emblematic of this type of discourse, the post-war Sartre

---

[4] [Preparatory class for the École normale supérieure. – Translator.]

5

– towards work of a different order. Foucault had a formula that I find very striking; he said that his work, in the end, was one of stripping away certain things that were self-evident, certain commonplaces. It seems to me that your view and Foucault's are very close in this respect. Isn't that a formula that you could apply to yourself?

PIERRE BOURDIEU: Quite so. I think that one point of total agreement between us is repudiation of the great figure of the 'total intellectual', as I call it, of whom Sartre was the embodiment par excellence, the intellectual who fulfils the role of prophet. Max Weber says that the prophet is the person who gives a total response to total questions, questions of life and death, and the like. And the philosopher, in his Sartrean incarnation, is a prophetic figure in the strict sense of the term, that is, responding globally to existential problems, problems of life, political problems, etc. For our generation, partly because we were somewhat overwhelmed and tired of this totalizing role, it was inconceivable to follow in Sartre's footsteps; to parody Malraux's formula, we did not want to issue the coin of the absolute.[5] In other words, no one can answer everything any more; you have to answer partial questions, questions deliberately constituted as partial, but answer these completely, or at least as completely as possible given the state of the instruments of knowledge. This kind of

---

[5] [A reference to André Malraux's *La Monnaie de l'absolu*, published in English as *The Twilight of the Absolute*, in which he argues that art has become a substitute for religion. – Translator.]

---

minimizing redefinition of the intellectual undertaking is, I believe, very important, as it is an advance in the direction of a greater seriousness, both scientifically and politically.

What I might add in relation to Foucault is that I have a rather activist conception of science, which doesn't at all mean the same as 'engaged'. Basically, I believe that social science, whether it is aware of this or not, whether it wishes to or not, responds to highly important questions; at any rate it raises these, and has the duty to raise them better than they are raised in the regular social world. For example, better than they are raised in the journalistic milieu, better than they are raised among essayists, better than they are raised in the milieu of false science.

ROGER CHARTIER: Are you not on somewhat dangerous ground in appealing to the notion of science? I read somewhere that you were spoken about as 'new-look Zhdanovism'.[6] How is it possible to constitute the definition of what one understands by science without falling back into the old habit of making distinctions 'scientifically' and 'institutionally' – because an authority was charged with imposing this distinction – between science and non-science?

---

[6] After Andrey Zhdanov (1896–1948), one of the top Soviet leaders of the 1940s. Zhdanovism is the doctrine that subordinated the arts and sciences to the ideological and political objectives of the Communist parties of the Stalin era. It particularly included the idea that scientific knowledge was pervaded by the class struggle, and opposed a (progressive) 'proletarian science' to a (reactionary) 'bourgeois science'.

PIERRE BOURDIEU: Yes, exactly, I think this is one of the major misunderstandings between myself – at least, between what I am trying to do – and many of my contemporaries, let's say people of my generation who were as it were born into intellectual and political life precisely in the epoch of Zhdanovism, and who at that time were Zhdanovists while I was anti-Zhdanovist – and I believe this was an important difference – who believed they could recognize in the work that sociology does what was practised under the name of science in the era of Stalinism, and particularly the break between science and ideology that I never adopted for myself, that I radically contest, as it is a mystical break and has been taken up – and not by chance – by philosophers and never by scientists, by practitioners of research. This break had a function quite analogous to that found in religious and prophetic discourses: it permitted a separation between the sacred and the profane, that is, those who are sacred and those who are profane, the (sacred) prophet and the profane. I find this detestable, I believe we are justified in speaking of science even if our science is inchoate, just beginning, hesitant, etc. Despite everything, there is a distinction in kind between the scientific effort made by the historian, the ethnologist, the sociologist or the economist, and what is done for example by the philosopher. We strive to be verifiable or falsifiable.

I can mention here an experience I had on the radio. One day, I came for a discussion with Lévy-Leboyer on his latest book about employers;[7] and I had myself just

---

[7] Maurice Lévy-Leboyer (ed.), *Le Patronat de la seconde industrialisation* (Paris: Éditions ouvrières, 1979).

---

written an article on this very topic. He arrived – I don't remember now if this was off the air or on – and said to me: 'You know, my dear colleague, I've seen your study, I've taken your figures, I've redone the statistics and we don't agree.' So I said to him: 'But how is that possible? How did you set up the problem?' 'Oh well, I didn't include bankers.' I said: 'Well then, that's the reason why we disagree.' So we discussed the construction of the object: is it possible to study employers without including bankers? That is a problem of scientific discussion, and subsequently he was able to redo the statistics and come to the same results as myself. This is the kind of thing that, it seems to me, allows me to speak of science, on the understanding that, when I say 'science', I mean that I can be refuted with scientific arguments. But up to now, that is still to be done.

I will take the opportunity to say something that means a lot to me: up till now, I have been the object of attacks, but never of refutations in the strict sense of the term; I might say that one thing that makes me sad is that in the French intellectual field I have many enemies but no opponents, that is, people who would do the work needed to present me with a refutation. I know that in such a case people will say: 'But if you're irrefutable, that's totalitarian.' Not at all. But they would have to be on their toes to refute me. That's a little arrogant, but still...

ROGER CHARTIER: No, don't worry, we won't flinch from the task. I believe that there is in your work, to get back to our starting-point, the desire to strip away certainties, as Foucault would put it. There is a phrase in *Questions de sociologie* that is very close to this:

'destroying verbal and mental automatisms',[8] accordingly, to make problematic what appears in the social world as taken for granted, all these distinctions that are declared as if they are self-evident, of the kind: 'It can't be otherwise, it's always been that way...' It seems to me that one of the most acute moves in your research is to show that the self-evident is always constructed, on the basis of the issues involved and their relative importance. And it is from this point of view, moreover, that historians and others can well benefit from your work as much as sociologists, in a relationship that is both supportive and critical, but also distant and respectful. That is, I believe, rather the sense of our present discussions. One of the ways in which, I believe, you took this stripping away of certainties farthest forward was in challenging boundaries, divisions and demarcations that are taken as natural whereas they are always socially constructed. We can say that in this perspective you are exemplary, because historians are now also confronted with what appear to be self-evident categories. To take some examples. One might believe that the distinction between young people and old belongs to nature – there are biologically, in fact, people who are young and people who are old; the same goes with regional boundaries – there clearly are administrative or territorial limits that mean you are in southern or northern France; or between social groups, with the objective categories produced by the INSEE[9] and other institutes

---

[8] Bourdieu, *Sociology in Question*, p. 70.
[9] [The Institut national de la statistique et des études économiques (INSEE) is the official French statistical service, also responsible for the national census. – Translator.]

that establish classifications meaning that there are middle classes, employers, wage-earners, and so on. For you, it is precisely these 'objective' divisions that have to be understood in terms of the historical dynamic that establishes them. It always needs to be asked, why this partition and not another, what and whom does it serve?

PIERRE BOURDIEU: I completely agree with what you've just said, and I believe that one of the contributions of my work – which is why I am always very surprised when it is described as dogmatic, terroristic, or what have you – has been to turn the scientific gaze on to science itself. For example, to take occupational classifications as the object of analysis instead of using them without hesitation or reflection. The paradox is that historians, for example – I believe we have the best school of historians in the world, and that's not just a formal compliment – often show an extraordinary naivety in their use of categories. For example, it is impossible to conduct longitudinal statistical studies comparing the status of medical doctors from the eighteenth century through to our day – perhaps I'm inventing this example – without being clear that the notion of a 'doctor' is a historical construction that has constantly changed. It is the very categories with which the historic object is constructed that should be the object of a historical analysis.

The same pertains in relation to the terms with which we speak about reality. 'Politics', for example, is completely a historically constituted notion, constituted very recently; the world of what I call the political field is practically an invention of the nineteenth century. You could discuss – I don't want to go out on a limb, being faced here with a redoubtable historian – but I believe that all these notions, all the words and concepts that we employ to conceptualize history, are themselves historically constituted; and strangely, historians are actually the most apt to fall into anachronism since, whether to seem modern or to make their work more interesting, or out of negligence, they employ words that are currently used to speak of realities within which these words were not current, or else had a different meaning. I believe that this reflexivity is extremely important.

ROGER CHARTIER: What you are saying about diachrony, the long term, that is, could also be said about the contemporary social world. The same words can be used by different groups, different milieus, and they don't have the same meaning. One of the pitfalls of this kind of approach, which consists in utilizing supposedly universal and invariant categories, is that it conceals the construction and historical variations of the object.

To return to the example of politics. I believe it is fundamental to show how the very definition of what is political is precisely the subject of least consensus. That is one of the points on which you have opposed statisticians or the professional opinion pollsters who deluge us all day long, when you show that the absence of responses has a meaning or that the same responses, when formulated at different places in society, have meanings that are completely incompatible.

PIERRE BOURDIEU: Yes, with sociologists the kind of anachronism that historians commit takes the form of a class ethnocentrism, that is, they tend to universalize the particular case: I take my own categories of thought, my systems of classification, my taxonomies, my divisions – into male/female, hot/cold, dry/wet, top/bottom, dominant class/dominated classes, etc. – and I universalize them. In the one case this produces anachronism, in the other case, ethnocentrism: in each case, it's a matter of not questioning one's own systems of questioning.

To come back then to my article 'The Categories of Professorial Understanding'; in fact, if I did have a theoretical model, it would be the Kantian one, which amounts to subjecting the instruments with which one conceives reality to reflexive critique. In my article, which I believe is the fullest illustration of it, I tried to determine the oppositions that professors apply in order to assess the work of a student or to judge their deceased colleagues – which moreover are the same ones. These categories of perception are also those with which they judge a book, they are those that they will unconsciously employ to read the books in which I analyse these categories. For example, it will be said: one of the obstacles to reading sociology is that sociology is plebeian. (I am using Cicero's old vocabulary, he spoke of *philosophia plebeia*.) It is not because it speaks of the people that sociology is plebeian, it is because it stands right at the bottom in the hierarchy of sciences. It also speaks more of the people than others, which is a point I shall come back to. But I believe that these categories of thought that are very deeply internalized are bound up with the hierarchy of disciplines in the educational system, where the pure disciplines like mathematics are 'higher' than the impure disciplines such as chemistry, or a fortiori geography; in the same way, philosophy is 'higher' than geography.

ROGER CHARTIER: History lies between the two.

PIERRE BOURDIEU: True, history is in the middle of the scale. These oppositions are extremely structuring and they even determine the selection of books, in other words what is published and what people write about. The more ambitious you are – which means, the more you are from a higher social origin and have a greater educational consecration – the more you take on vast subjects: global, ecumenical, theoretical, and so on. All these things that intellectuals should objectivize actually manipulate the thinking of intellectuals. Someone who discloses this, not at all to annoy other people but simply as a check on himself, is disturbing. Almost by definition.

ROGER CHARTIER: I would say that he also disturbs himself, since the writing then becomes extremely tense, extremely complex. If someone thinks as a historian, on the basis of what you said, about this tension between words, which may remain invariant, and notions that are constructed either chronologically or socially, in extremely varied ways, what are they doing? There are many possible choices and I don't think any one of them is totally satisfactory. Either the historian duplicates the language of the actors themselves, and there is an entire wing of the French historical school that has tried to write history in the categories and vocabulary of the times and people whose history they are telling. Or else they translate, that is, everything is transposed from one time into another. Paul Veyne, when he wants to have people understand the Roman world, to show the radical difference that separates it from our own, translates everything. But it is precisely by way of this effect of forced and alien familiarity that he seeks to show the differences. Or else historians apply a concept born at a given moment, in a particular historical circumstance, to other older realities, in order to test that concept, but also to show this older reality in a more striking fashion.

We can take the example of *A History of Private Life* published under the editorship of Duby and Ariès, who has sadly since died. It is clear that the concept of 'private life' cannot be taken as contemporary with the medieval period or the sixteenth century. It is a concept whose definitions are either earlier, for example in Roman law, or else later, with the concept of 'privacy' (in the English-speaking world) that denotes the reduced intimacy of the nineteenth century, centred on family affectivity. Historians have even taken sides and banked on being able to make this notion function, over a very long period of time, despite its being anachronistic in many situations, so as to try and test historical realities that could be perceived in a new fashion, and at the same time to test this notion, to show the limits of its pertinence. But in every case the choice is extremely difficult, and I suppose the same is true for the sociologist working on the contemporary social world. The tension and the complexity encountered in your writings or in those of other sociologists, sometimes to the point of obscurity, seems to me to follow from this difficulty. How is it possible to account for the variation in a vocabulary that seems stable because we have inherited it from a certain historical moment?

PIERRE BOURDIEU: Indeed, everything you have said as a historian, I could subscribe to as a sociologist.

I was going to say 'a fortiori', because very often we come back to the opposition between past and present; the present is not the temporal present, it is what is still sufficiently alive to be the object of struggles; and at this particular point in time, for example, the French Revolution can be very present. But we ourselves are always among the living, and what we speak of is always an object of contention; and so the very words that we use to speak of what we are speaking of are objects of struggle, and are used differently by political actors. For example, one of the principles of political struggle is to struggle for common words: for example, who is a republican? Everyone is a republican; at election times people talk of republican discipline, republican solidarity, etc. Everyone is in the centre... In short, there are words that we know owe their price in the struggle to the fact that they are objects of struggle. And for us, speaking of these struggles and in all the spheres that I call 'fields' – these kinds of little arenas where we play different games: whether the scientific field, the political field or the field of historians, the field of sociologists, or what have you – in each of these worlds there will be keywords like this over which people fight.

How should all this be described? Clearly there is a weapon, which is the quotation mark. Bachelard magnificently said about the natural sciences, but it is true a fortiori for the social sciences: 'Science is a matter of quotation marks.' I say the same thing, but emphasizing that it is not I who am speaking, I am marking a distance of objectivation. This is something that creates misunderstandings about what I am saying. When I say, for example: 'The dominated classes prefer Dalida'[10] – that's not a good example, I should perhaps give better examples – people think that I think this. The sociologist spends his time recording value judgements as facts. In the domain of culture, for example, I record as a fact that there are cultural works that are more legitimate than others, and it turns out that very often they are the works I like best. But that said, I do not make a value judgement. I say: try and put an essay in praise of Dalida on the educational market, and you'll get zero marks; whereas if you offer a shabby little praise of Johann Sebastian Bach, you'll get an average result. There, that's a social fact. And this is very poorly understood; it is one of the points of distance that is very much bound up with quotation marks. Then the problem of writing is a nightmare, and very often I have problems because people think I am imposing some kind of orthodoxy...

If I have a minute, what I would like to say is that the relationship of the sociologist to his work and his writing corresponds completely to the description that is given of schizophrenia, as far as I am familiar with this. Something has to be said, or something done, and at the time when it is said or done, you have to say that you are not doing what you have just said or done, and in a third discourse, to say again that you are not doing what you have just said you are doing, and so on. In other words,

---

[10] [Dalida (1933–87) was a very popular Franco-Italian singer who had a thirty-year career. In a poll published in 1988 in *Le Monde* she was voted second (behind General de Gaulle) among those individuals who had the greatest impact on French society. – Translator.]

---

there is a series of levels of discourse that make language impossible, so much so that, for example, part of what I've done could be summed up by the most stupid of Marxist slogans: 'The dominant culture is the culture of the dominant class.' I can actually say that all my work is constructed against what this phrase both says and does not say, but at the same time it does not invalidate this phrase because, by and large, what it says remains true, but so generally that it is false. The same analysis could be applied to the notion of 'ideology'. The notion of ideology is clearly an instrument of struggles: ideology is other people's science, other people's thinking, etc. And at the same time, the fact of having said that there is ideology, that is, discourses produced on the basis of an effort to legitimize one's own position, this was an important scientific achievement. That said, my own work has been 90 per cent constructed against this notion of ideology; and all my efforts to talk about symbolic power, symbolic domination, misrecognition and so on, to introduce a heap of things that could be described as a complicated jargon, were necessary in order to preserve a distinction, a gain that is, moreover, often bound up with Marxism in its original and combative form. I needed to both preserve and destroy at the same time, which led to an extremely difficult effort that is located both within language and in the very construction of sentences; it is a discourse carrying a metadiscourse that constantly says 'Be careful what you read.' And unfortunately, I have not obtained from my contemporaries the reading I expected. I do obtain it, but not at all among the people who write in newspapers.

2

Illusions and Knowledge

ROGER CHARTIER: You say in your book *Questions de sociologie* that 'any advance in the knowledge of necessity is an advance in possible freedom'. This seems to offer a good beginning for a second exchange, devoted to another break with the past that your work proposes in relation to the classic role attributed to intellectuals. It could be said that for a long time the role of intellectuals was that of imposing on the dominated the discourse expected of them regarding their own condition, therefore imposing on them a discourse that they were not able to establish by themselves but that others developed for them. It seems to me that in your perspective, which has this heuristic ability of leading thought into other domains than that of sociology, the project is completely different, since what is involved here is providing tools that make it possible to dismantle the mechanisms of domination that operate as natural divisions – normal and ancestral. We have here a project that proposes the individual retaking possession of himself – something that, I believe, is quite opposed to a stereotyped image of your work, which is conceived as laying bare the constraints against which nothing can be done, and which crush individuals by not giving them any space.

PIERRE BOURDIEU: If I wanted to reply to what you have just said in a single sentence, I would say: we are born determined and we have a small chance of ending up free; we are born into the unthought and we have a very small chance of becoming subjects. I criticize those people who are always invoking freedom, the subject, the person, etc. for enclosing social agents in the illusion of freedom, which is one of the ways by which determinism is exercised. And out of all social categories (this is a sociological paradox and no doubt one of the things that causes my work to upset intellectuals), the category most inclined to the illusion of freedom is that of intellectuals. It is in this sense, for example, that Sartre – whatever the merits we acknowledge in him – was the ideologist of the intellectuals, that is, the one who cultivated the illusion of the intellectual 'without attachments or roots', as Mannheim put it, the illusion of consciousness of self, the illusion that the intellectual can master his own truth. And I believe that, in the frantic refusal with which some people oppose sociology, when they denounce its supposed 'hatred of philosophy', there is this refusal to reveal the intellectual as caught up in specific determinisms: those of categories of thought, of mental structures, of academic loyalties and attachments, which moreover often have a far more deforming effect than political attachments. I believe that academics are led far more by academic interests than by political interests. In other words, I believe that appropriating the instruments of thought, and also the objects of thought that one receives, is a condition of possibility for becoming to a small extent the subject of one's thoughts; one is not born the subject of one's thoughts, one becomes their subject, on condition, among other things – I believe that there are other instruments; there is also psychoanalysis, for example – of reappropriating the knowledge of determinisms. I believe that I do exactly the opposite of what people have me as saying in this case.

ROGER CHARTIER: Yes, but doesn't this lead to the kind of terrifying paradox that amounts to saying that you write for people who can't read you and you are read by those who don't want to understand you?

PIERRE BOURDIEU: True. I believe that they can't understand me because they don't want to understand me. I mentioned just now Deguy's essay 'La haine de la philosophie',[1] which I find quite touching. This text is an extraordinary document on the suffering that culture can provoke, and that analysis, in the sense of socio-analysis, can provoke: analysis of the relationship to culture that obsesses all educated people. I am perfectly familiar with Deguy's suffering. And if people had read *Distinction* right through, instead of reducing it to absurd simplifications, they would have seen, in a post-script where I refer to Proust, that I mention both the specific pleasures that the relationship to culture gives and the specific sufferings that cultural disenchantment

---

[1] In Michel Deguy, *Choses de la poésie et affaire culturelle* (Paris: Hachette, 1986).

---

induces. Proust was an admirable sociologist, and he said before me, but in his own language – meaning that no one understood him – what *Distinction* says.

ROGER CHARTIER: Why is it that from the appearance of *Distinction*, which was published in 1979, we've had this whole series of mechanisms of rejection and reduction of your work to a few slogans? Your earlier publications on the educational system had met with both support and criticism, but they did not unleash the same type of reaction. People might dispute their fundamental concepts, such as 'reproduction', for example, or raise objections to your argument, but without violent denunciation. And conversely, these works were founding texts in the historical sociology of education, offering instruments and methods that historians needed so as to experiment on a terrain that was differently constructed from the contemporary educational system. Why did *Distinction* lead to such a violent debate? The word 'debate' is actually not the right one, as we're not really talking about discussion but rather about stigmatization.

PIERRE BOURDIEU: I think that culture in our societies is a sacred site: the religion of culture has become, for certain social categories including intellectuals, the site of their deepest convictions and commitments. For example, the shame of committing a cultural gaffe has become the equivalent of sin. I believe that the analogy with religion can be pushed quite far. And whereas today an analysis of religious sociology such as the one I wrote on the bishops doesn't bother anyone, not even bishops (I have even had eminent bishops as students, for example, who would have been able to write, or should have been able to write, what I myself wrote about bishops),[2] the sociology of culture suddenly comes up against amazing resistances. If you think of the work of objectivation that is done on religion: everyone knows today, and no one can challenge this, that there is a certain correlation between the religion acquired in one's family and the religion one professes; no one can deny that there is a transmission of religious convictions from father to son, and that, when this transmission dies out, so too does religion. These are things that everyone acknowledges. But when someone says this about culture, it amounts to taking away from the cultivated man one of the foundations of the charm of culture, which is the illusion of innateness, the charismatic illusion: I acquired it by myself, by birth, it's like a kind of miracle. All these things explain the violent resistance. It's very surprising.

Finally, my conviction is that sociology is a way of continuing philosophy by other means. If I wanted to give sociology a glorious genealogy, I would say that basically the first sociologist was Socrates. Philosophers will be furious, as they claim this founding father. But indeed, he clearly was someone who went into the street and asked questions, who asked an Athenian general what courage was, who asked Euthyphron, a pious man, what piety was, and so on. He conducted surveys, up to a certain point. And to go back to what you were just saying about the struggle against representations, he was someone who struggled for a long time against the equivalent of my opponents today – no, not my

---

[2] Bourdieu and de Saint Martin, 'La sainte famille: L'épiscopat français dans le champ du pouvoir'.

---

opponents but my enemies, or in any case those I combat scientifically – that is, the sophists: people who at the same time speak of an unreal entity that they would have people believe is real, and shift the real into the distance by a cloud of impressive words, etc.

If I claim this authority, it is not simply a strategic stroke in order to appropriate a noble ancestor. For example, there is all the work I have done against those whom I call the 'doxosophists' – a word I borrowed from Plato: it's a magnificent word; *doxa* means both opinion, belief and also representation, seeming, semblance; and *sophos* means a person who knows. The doxosophists are at the same time scholars of appearance and seeming scholars. As I see it, the people who produce opinion polls, for example, are the equivalent of sophists today, that is, people who are given money (the sophists made people pay, Socrates was hardly paid), honours, profits, material profits, symbolic profits, etc., in order to produce a semblance of the social world which everyone knows at bottom is false but which has an extraordinary force to it, owing to the fact that it makes it possible to obscure certain truths about the social world.

Then I basically come to the real response: the problem of the sociologist is that he tries to say things that no one wants to know, and especially not those who read him. And by the same token, this sometimes makes me doubt the legitimacy of my existence as a sociologist and the function of scientific work; is it good to say what is true about the social world? Would it be possible to live in a social world that knew itself? I believe the answer is yes. I think that many kinds of suffering, many kinds of misery, which are always forgotten by the great

Marxist denunciation, would be tremendously attenuated, even transformed or abolished, if there was a transparency, a greater knowledge of how things stand in matters of culture, of religion, of work, and so on.

ROGER CHARTIER: But aren't we close here to a kind of utopianism? I think this is a word you have sometimes used. How, in fact, could one ensure the divulging of tools that could enable people to become aware of determinations, and hence make room for a small margin of freedom? Isn't there also a risk of populism in deeming it necessary to break with all immediate knowledge or a whole inherited culture in order to bring to the dominated tools of rational analysis that strip away, dismantle, deconstruct what makes up reality itself?

PIERRE BOURDIEU: Yes, there are two things. There is populism, which is one thing; and then there is this kind of stripping-away radicalism, which is something else. The two don't necessarily go together. As far as populism is concerned, I do not believe that I've left the least room for ambiguity. Here again, I could use a Socratic metaphor: Socrates questions, but he does not take the answers he is given as legal tender. And the sociologist knows very well that people who give answers in perfectly good faith do not necessarily speak the truth. His whole work consists in constructing the conditions for elaborating truth on the basis of the observed behaviours, of discourses, writings, etc. Even if there are always a few imbeciles who believe that the common people speak more truly than others. In fact, one aspect of the people being particularly dominated is that they are particularly dominated by the symbolic mechanisms of domination. For example, anyone who thinks (this was the fashion at the time the left was in power) that putting a microphone in front of the mouth of a miner will gather the truth about miners; in fact, what you get are the trade union discourses of the last thirty years; and when you do the same with a farmer, you get the discourses of schoolteachers – transformed. So the idea that you could find a kind of place of original insight in the social world, whether this is the intellectuals, or the proletariat, or some other group, is one of those mystiques that have enabled intellectuals to give themselves a boost, but on the basis of a dramatic self-mystification. The sociologist listens, questions, has people speak, but he also gives himself the means of subjecting every discourse to criticism. That goes without saying within the profession, but I think it is not known outside of it.

The second problem is, can this science that is destructive of accepted ideas – and here, moreover, sociology is very close to the writing of people like Flaubert; the analogy is tremendous; what is a problem for me is that this is not perceived, that people accept from Flaubert what they detest in Bourdieu, whereas for me it's the same thing... Can this science that is destructive of accepted ideas itself escape being challenged in the same way? Sociology objectivizes everything; can it objectivize itself? And if it objectivizes itself, does it not destroy its own foundations? This is an old argument, as old as social science, and it amazes me that people still dare to formulate it except in the *terminale* class, that they formulate it in a scientific debate. In the end, however, it demands a response: given that the historian is himself part of history, is there a science of history? Given that the sociologist is himself in society, is there a science of sociology? Here I believe that an answer is possible, it simply takes a bit of time. I shall try to argue this in a couple of sentences. I believe that sociological discourse is generated in a space that is itself a social space, in a scientific field where there are struggles, competition, and so on, and, as in the natural sciences, a certain advance towards greater knowledge is possible by way of a struggle among people seeking to appropriate knowledge of the social world, on condition that this struggle is subject to the minimal rules of regulated dialogue. In other words, on condition that not all blows are permitted. For example, on condition that a scientific argument cannot be quashed by a political argument. It is impossible to kill a mathematical theorem by saying that it's right wing, but it is possible to kill a sociological or historical theory by saying that it's right wing. A relatively autonomous scientific field, capable of producing provisional truths backed up by verifications, is a field in which this kind of blow is no longer possible. Unfortunately this is not the case; sociologists find it hard to guard their world against the irruption of playground arguments.

ROGER CHARTIER: Perhaps my question wasn't that of a *terminale* essay...

PIERRE BOURDIEU: Well I certainly didn't have you in mind, you know that! (*Laughter.*)

ROGER CHARTIER: You are one of the people who drew attention in France to the work of the English sociologist Richard Hoggart, who wrote his magnificent book

The Uses of Literacy in the 1950s. He tried to show how, in relation to all the dominant discourses broadcast by mass culture (newspapers, television, radio), those who were subject to these messages, far from being completely dominated or destroyed by them, always maintained in relation to them what is called in translation *'attention oblique'* ['oblique attention'] or *'adhésion à éclipses'* ['sporadic adherence']. Do you not believe that the tools that the sociologist's critical discourse would propose as weapons making it possible for the most dominated, the most deprived, to regain possession, risk appearing in their own turn as projects from outside, and thus finding themselves subject to the same sporadic adherence, the same oblique attention? Which means, in the end, doesn't the critique of the conditions of domination risk appearing as itself forming part of domination? How can spontaneous knowledge of the social world, which is certainly made up of these attitudes of defiance and defence, be imbued with a critical reflection and appropriate theoretical tools enabling it to take a distance from social determinisms?

PIERRE BOURDIEU: Once again, I believe that we have two questions here. I believe that what sociology produces, at least sociology as I conceive it, are instruments of self-defence against symbolic aggression, against symbolic manipulation, that is, essentially against the professional producers of discourse. And it is clear that the sociologist cannot count, as I have said several times, on the producers of symbols, that is, on journalists, bishops, teachers, philosophers, in fact on all those whose profession is to speak and to speak about the social world, since a considerable part of his work consists in warning against the rhetoric of everyday discourse about the social world, the discourse of the semi-wise. The problem is that the instruments of self-defence that the sociologist produces – he teaches a symbolic judo – are intercepted by people who make use of them, and, take my word for it, sociology enters into a large part of advertising, a large part of marketing...

For example, you could take a certain evening's television, an election night, and make a tremendous analysis of it, but an unpublishable one because it would be viewed as a criminal demolition: you would see the professor of political science commenting on the journalist who then comments on the politician, each struggling not to have the last word but to be in a position of metadiscourse in relation to the previous speaker. To offer a very amusing metaphor, there was a famous experiment by the Kelloggs, who worked on chimpanzees.[3] One day, they hung a banana in the air out of reach of an ordinary chimpanzee; all the apes tried to jump up to it, and then Sultan, who was the cleverest, seized a small female chimp, one of his girlfriends, set her down, climbed on top of her and captured the banana. Then all the chimpanzees tried to copy him, with one paw in the air and trying to climb on top of another one, but they wouldn't cooperate any more. They'd all understood that you mustn't let anyone climb on top of you, no one wanted to be underneath. And in many of the discussions that we see on television, election night debates, etc., what you have is people climbing up with their paw in the air, but to get what? To be the one in the 'meta'

---

[3] W. N. Kellogg and L. A. Kellogg, *The Ape and the Child* [1933] (New York: Hafner, 1967).

---

position: 'I'm going to tell you what saying what you are saying means.' You have the regular historian – I won't name him here, but everyone knows who he is[4] – who steps up and says: 'Yes, if we compare the statistics of such and such years, it seems that what might appear a victory is not a victory but rather a defeat, up to a certain point. And so on.' And then someone else will climb on top of him. To point out this kind of mechanism, I believe, would be tremendously useful. But who is interested in broadcasting it? He will be intercepted, as they say in rugby, before getting to the wing. And as you were just saying, the people who would have an interest in hearing these kinds of things have only the slightest chance of hearing them.

That said, they have spontaneous defence systems that should not be underestimated; they have instruments of passive resistance – for example, that of going off to make a sandwich during the programme – but also active ones. There is one example that I always give, about the '*participation*' that de Gaulle proposed, an extraordinary expression that I heard from a worker at Renault: 'What participation means is "Lend me your watch and I'll tell you the time".' It's even (*laughter*): 'Give me your watch and I'll tell you the time.' This isn't a political analysis, and to develop what is contained in this kind of metaphorical or parabolic message, you would need hours of analysis. But yes, there are instruments of defence. If the instruments of defence produced by advanced science and the instruments of spontaneous

---

[4] Bourdieu is referring to the historian René Rémond (1918–2007), for many years *the* academic commentator on French television on election nights.

defence came together... that is, if you had rugby players who saw the match on a video recorder and could make use of it, you would have a profound change in political life. You would make life impossible for the sophists; but that won't happen tomorrow, as, for the time being, the sophists control the broadcasts.

ROGER CHARTIER: Is that why you supported Coluche's candidacy?[5]

---

[5] On 30 October 1980, the comedian Coluche announced that he would be a 'candidate for candidacy' in the presidential election due to be held the following May: 'I call on the lazy, the dirty, drug addicts, alcoholics, queers, women, parasites, the young, the old, jailbirds, dykes, apprentices, Blacks, pedestrians, Arabs, French, the hairy, the mad, transvestites, former Communists, convinced abstentionists, all those whom politicians leave out of the count, to vote for me, put their name on the voters' list and spread the news: All together to kick them in the butt with Coluche. The only candidate with no reason to lie!' Though polls gave Coluche between 10 and 16 per cent of voting intentions, he came under a number of different pressures. On 16 April 1981, he announced his withdrawal. Pierre Bourdieu commented on the episode in 1999 in the following terms: 'When a simple citizen is told that he is politically irresponsible, he is accused of illegally practising politics. One of the virtues of these irresponsible people – of whom I am one – is that they bring to light a tacit presupposition of the political order, precisely that lay people are excluded from it. Coluche's candidacy was one of these irresponsible acts. [...] The whole media-political field was mobilized, across all political differences, to condemn the downright barbarity of questioning the fundamental presupposition that only politicians are allowed to talk about politics.' (Pierre Bourdieu, 'Politics Belongs to Them', in Bourdieu, *Political Interventions*, pp. 124–5.)

PIERRE BOURDIEU: It's not unconnected. I believe that Coluche's candidacy was completely serious, as he made a practical challenge, by derision, etc., without any Poujadiste[6] element...That's something quite remarkable. Here we have an example of defence...There were very scholarly articles, obviously in *Le Monde* – a very, very scholarly paper – saying that this was the rebirth of Poujadism, or what have you. But I had statistics showing that Coluche had a social base that was the very opposite of the regular base of Poujadism, in fact intellectuals, young people with educational qualifications higher than the jobs they could obtain with them, in other words the traditional base of the left. Coluche is interesting because what he created in practice were critical 'happenings'. I'll use a more elevated image, at the opposite pole in the hierarchical space of culture, that of Karl Kraus. No one in France has read him, but everyone knows they are supposed to say that Kraus was very good. So I shall make use of this legitimacy effect. (*Laughter.*) Karl Kraus was a professional intellectual who spent his life doing, basically, the opposite of what Sartre did. He spent his life doing 'happenings'. He did wonderful things, and if I had the time I would do the same. He drew up mock petitions on the basis of the sentiments of good social behaviour that inspire intellectuals: good causes. Today, for example, it would be the defence of homosexuals, against AIDS, etc. He drew up a mock petition signed by the most famous

---

[6] ['Poujadism' was a 1950s movement of shopkeepers and managers of small businesses against income tax and price control, led by Pierre Poujade, owner of a stationer's and bookstore in the Lot department. – Translator.]

names of the day, and people didn't dare give it the lie. Later, he revealed that he had invented the whole thing, that these people hadn't signed. This man spent his life doing theatrical 'happenings' in the same style as Coluche, chaotic events in which he challenged this whole world of the sophists. And so much could be done to spread this kind of practical defence.

ROGER CHARTIER: Yes, but they will say once again that you are looking for a stick to beat yourself with...

PIERRE BOURDIEU: Clearly, my own temperament is largely responsible for that – what people call 'temperament' and what I call 'habitus'. I've presented things in an exaggerated form in order to extend the question. But what I do think is that there is a place for a rational utopianism, in other words, that we have the right to a portion of utopia within the limits of the possible. And I believe that a good use of sociology as an instrument for the transformation of the social world would be to define the limits of what can be done and to go as far as possible beyond these limits with just a small chance of success.

ROGER CHARTIER: Isn't one of these limits in that sentence from Ecclesiastes that you cite somewhere: 'Who increases knowledge increases pain'? In the end, in other words, the laying bare of all the mechanisms of domination, now that people have abandoned the idea that this domination could be transformed with a kind of hope for a brand-new day, a kind of messianism that would subvert the whole of the social world and recreate it on new foundations, is perhaps more the source of a kind of despair than of a great political project. Because another of the ruptures with the traditional figure of the intellectual, at least the one that emerged from the Second World War, is the loss of the illusion that the steady accumulation of all frustrations into a kind of cumulative movement would lead to a great rupture. No one believes this any more. And so, from this moment on, doesn't the work of laying bare, in the absence of any messianic hope, produce an endless increase in pain? And isn't that an obstacle, more fundamental than those that you have described, to an appropriation of the instruments of criticism?

PIERRE BOURDIEU: I think that messianic hope is one of the great obstacles to transformations. We have to substitute for this messianic illusion rational hopes that are completely moderate, which are often discredited as reformist, as compromises, etc., whereas these actually come in very, very radical forms. For example, what I said just now, which led to my being treated as utopian, as rather irresponsible, is rational! I believe that if intellectuals all worked in the space that concerned them to bring about a little bit of transparency, a bit less self-mystification, this would be a great change. To take a very simple measure: if there were a legally guaranteed commission of sociologists, lawyers, and so on, to control the proper use of opinion polls – not only the sample size, it would go far beyond this – that would be progress in the direction of democracy; that's a very simple example. Now this is something that would be seen as unworthy of being demanded. Instead we should concern ourselves with Vietnam, that is, with things which are completely out of reach, which, as the Stoics say, do not depend on us. What we need to see is what does depend on us. And the things that depend on us are basically far more important than people believe. For example, everything that is mystification produced by intellectuals is something that depends on us. That is why the critique of the intellectual illusion, which is our responsibility – not that this is in any way the be-all and end-all of political action – is undoubtedly the most important thing that we can do. There are many other things to do; but what depends on us, fundamentally, is that.

3

Structures and the Individual

ROGER CHARTIER: It seems to me that the social sciences – sociology, history, anthropology – are currently all occupied with the attempt to resolve a dilemma (which is perhaps a false problem anyway) between what dominated them in the 1960s, that is, approaches in terms of structures, hierarchies, objective positions, and, on the other hand, all those attempts which may take different forms in each of these disciplines, and focus on different objects, but have in common the desire to restore the actions, strategies and representations of individuals and the relationships that connect them. It is clear that in history, after the dominance of a social history aiming at exhibiting the objective hierarchies of a society, discovered on the basis of taxation and legal data and combined in global patterns, we are now geared to approaches that seek to conceive the roles of subjects. Hence the return to biography, the return to intentionality, or indeed the use of notions such as that of 'community', which has become so important among historians who no longer want to think in terms of occupational categories or social classes.

I believe that this tension exists not only in history, but also in sociology. In the last book that you published, *Choses dites*, there is an interview[1] that takes up this opposition – between structuralist approaches and all those others that have something in common with phenomenology, whether they are called interactionism, ethnomethodology or whatever – but only to declare it false or ineffective. It seems to me that for you – this is perhaps a path of reflection that we could pursue in this interview – these oppositions are largely false problems, but are none the less essential because they allow people readily to stand out and present an easy image of originality and innovation, while others, who remain loyal to structures, are dismissed as traditional or archaic. First of all, however, why do you think that the tension between structural approaches and phenomenological approaches is not a false problem?

PIERRE BOURDIEU: There is a whole skein of problems in what you've just said. First of all, on the idea of false revolutions that you mentioned: if these false sociological problems, false scientific problems, persist, this is because they are often based on real social problems or on real social interests. For example, as you suggested, I believe that the majority of these oppositions between macro and micro, objective and subjective, and today, among historians, between economic

---

[1] 'Répères', interview with Johan Heilbron and Benjo Maso, in Bourdieu, *Choses dites*, pp. 47–71 [*In Other Words*, pp. 34–54].

analysis and political analysis, and so on, are false oppositions that do not resist three seconds of theoretical analysis, but that they are extremely important because they fulfil social functions for those who use them. For example, the scientific field unfortunately obeys laws of change that are completely similar to that of haute couture or that of the religious field. In other words, young people, new arrivals, start revolutions, create heresies, either real or pretend, and say: 'Look, the oldies have all bored us for thirty years with economic history in the style of Labrousse and Braudel: we counted the barrels in the port of Lisbon, etc. That's enough! Now we have to count something else.' Then they count books, for example, in the same way that they counted barrels, without bothering too much about what these books contained. Or else they say: 'But no, all that belongs to politics.' That's exactly the same as dresses that are longer one year and shorter the year after...

The interest of false problems is that they are eternal. Besides, from the point of view of science, these false problems are often rooted in real political problems: that's the case, for example, with the opposition between individuals and society, individualism and socialism, individualism and holism, all those 'ism' words that I see as absurd, without any sense. These oppositions can always be reactivated because they have something to do with the opposition between collectivism or socialism on the one hand and liberalism on the other. And by way of these underground affiliations, political struggles can be brought into the scientific field. Now, the autonomy of the scientific field depends on the establishment of frontiers against these false problems. For example, a position that is scientifically very weak can be strengthened if it has political forces behind it. In a period of advanced liberalism, you have a rise in the assets of all those who hold to the absurd theory of *Homo economicus*. A rise in certain milieus, not in scientific practice, but a rise all the same. Suddenly it is possible to conduct an operation in the scientific field with the help of a political conjuncture.

Now, why are these problems false problems? That's another story, as they say. It's extremely hard, but I shall try to put it very concretely. First of all, there is Durkheim's idea that sociology is difficult because we all see ourselves as sociologists. One of the particular difficulties of sociology – but it's the same thing with history – lies in the fact that we believe we're already imbued with science; we believe we understand immediately, and one of the obstacles to understanding is this illusion of immediate comprehension. One of the ways to break with this illusion is to objectivize it. So we get that famous sentence which was like a thunderclap in the world of science: 'Social facts must be treated as things.' It is necessary to act as if, where Roger Chartier (or Pierre Bourdieu) is concerned, I should study him as if he had no subjectivity, without attaching importance to what he tells me, to his lived experience, to what he tells me of his mental experiences and his representations. Not only do I make a clean slate of all that, but I actually distrust it. This is all what Durkheim called 'prenotions', what Marx called 'ideologies', or spontaneous sociology; no matter, I distrust it. I record it, but I distrust it. That is the objectivist position.

ROGER CHARTIER: In order to move towards the objective properties that could adequately describe the individual...

PIERRE BOURDIEU: Correct. This is generally where statistics is brought in. Someone says, for example: I shall count the number of times that Roger Chartier says *'allons'*, because that will reveal something that he does not know himself but that is more important than anything he has told me. I shall measure the position of his voice; these are things that have been done, it is possible to predict someone's social position from such things as the position of the voice in the throat. There, that's objectivism. On the other side, people say: what's interesting is what subjects think, their representations, their discourses, their mental images; what they have in their heads about the social world. And you have to make an effort, either of self-analysis (that's a form of phenomenology) or to help others to self-analysis; in the end, to collect their representations, their discourse, etc.

All this is an absolutely stupid opposition that I think I can destroy in a single sentence. I could do the same for society/individual, which in any case is very close to this. A sentence from Pascal sums it up very well. I am simplifying it a bit, to put it in my own way (to quote it literally, which I could do, would only have a fetish value): 'The world comprehends me, but I comprehend it.' He plays on the word 'comprehend'. The world comprehends me and annihilates me as a point; I am a thing in the world; I am so as a body; I am located, dated, determined; I am subject to its forces; if I jump out of the window I fall under the law of gravity. And

I comprehend it, that is, I have representations of it and I am not reducible to the position that I occupy in this world. What does this mean? It means that, as soon as we take as object this quite particular thing that is man, we have to take into account this double reality existing in objectivity. He is a thing; he can be weighed, measured, counted; we can list his properties, how many books, cars, etc. he has. And then it is also part of the objectivity that he represents these things to himself. Each one of us has a point of view: this is located in a social space and sees the social space from this point in the social space. Once you've said this, it is quite clear that the alternative is idiotic. To understand Roger Chartier's point of view on history, you have to know where Roger Chartier is located in the space of historians. And you will have both the objective truth of Roger Chartier and the explanation of his representations. The work of the sociologist is to encompass the two things. It's exactly the same for the individual and for society. This completely fictitious opposition is very useful, as it can be applied either in an objectivist or in a subjectivist sense. In my youth I was fortunate enough to construct a position for myself both with Sartre and Lévi-Strauss and against both Sartre and Lévi-Strauss. The one, Sartre, embodied the subjectivist position in its most radical form, and the other, Lévi-Strauss, embodied the objectivist position in its most radical form. And this means that there was no sense in saying that you agreed with either one or the other. You agreed with one against the other and with the other against the first.

ROGER CHARTIER: Do you not believe that in each biographical trajectory there is a moment or a place that makes it possible, not to become aware of the foolishness of this opposition, but to bring into play a certain number of instruments with a view to overcoming it. For you, it seems to me that it was through your ethnological work, particularly on Béarn, that is, on your own identity, your own community of origin, that this resolution was made – at least a provisional and always difficult one, since it is not necessarily the same sources or the same instruments that are applied in research, depending on the point of view that you adopt. At a given moment, because there is an extreme situation, which is not the usual case in research but directly involves the individual in a society that is also his own, something is triggered. What has always struck me, reading the studies that you did on Kabylia and still more on Béarn and the problem of matrimonial strategies, is that they give an exemplary expression of what you want to show here, that is, the absurdity of the opposition between objectivity and subjectivity when one is oneself in a situation of 'epistemological experimentation' – I believe that is the expression you used. That doesn't necessarily happen every day.

PIERRE BOURDIEU: I think that the propensity towards objectivism or subjectivism is unevenly strong depending on the object, and depending on the relationship between the knowing subject and the object that is in the process of being known. For example, I think that the situation of the ethnologist is conducive to objectivism: the fact of being foreign – the phenomenological tradition has reflected a good deal on this situation of foreignness – of being someone who is outside of the game, who has no stake in the games he observes, who describes for example matrimonial strategies without having any personal interest in these things, is conducive to an objectivist view. The same holds for a sociologist studying a system of education: in no way does he behave like a father looking for the best establishment of higher education for his son. For example, when I was working on the *grandes écoles*, I sought to objectify, to make visible, mechanisms that were completely unconscious, that escaped the consciousness both of the students who were enrolling there, who ran around like laboratory rats in a maze, and of the people who advised them. The advisers themselves did not know what they were advising, which does not mean that their advice was no good. I was trying to do something completely objectivist. That was of no use to me as advice regarding the best school for my own son. In any case, I am not in the same position. I have a kind of disinterestedness that is constitutive of the situation. Which does not mean that I don't have an interest, but this is an interest of a different kind.

The impossible situations of epistemological experimentation in which I have deliberately put myself on two occasions are, on the one hand, the study of a village in which I spent the whole of my childhood and in which the people whom I was studying were friends whom I knew well, and, on the other hand, the study of the university that I did a few years ago. In both of these cases, even if I was able to abandon myself to the objectivist temptation, at a certain moment the object itself would necessarily have referred me to my subjective interests. For example, when you analyse the academic system, you bring out hierarchies that have different principles. You show that the university world is divided around the struggle over two possible principles of hierarchy. On the one hand, to be top in terms of power over the instruments of reproduction: to be president of an *agrégation* jury, to be president of a CNU[2] section, that is, being capable of reproducing oneself, or controlling reproduction, or preventing the reproduction of others; and then, on the other hand, reputation: the fact of being translated into foreign languages, of being invited by noble institutions, of having a Nobel prize, for example. These two principles of hierarchical ordering exist in a state of competition. In a certain sense, what is very interesting is that the sociologist, by way of objective techniques, that is, without referring to people's opinions, produces hierarchies and, once these are reproduced, they appear as self-evident. Everyone says: 'We knew this, it was obvious.' And at the same time, a tremendous effort is needed to counter all the accepted ideas and render this hierarchy objective, to put it on paper.

So it is very clear that there is a gap: as a native here, I indignantly observe heaps of practices whose purpose is a collective effort to hide these self-evident things, to deny these hierarchies that everyone acknowledges. This is a case where you need both representations in order to give a good description of the academic world: there are hierarchies, and no one wants to know them. That's still too simple: there are collective mechanisms, socially instituted, that function as defence systems in the Freudian sense, that is, that make it

---

[2] The Conseil national des universités, which decides on the recruitment and career of research teachers.

possible not to see these hierarchies. Why? Perhaps because the world of the university and scholarship would be unliveable if objective truth became subjective truth. I was faced with this kind of question in a less dramatic manner in studying employers and bishops, where this problem exists as well.

ROGER CHARTIER: But you imply by this that historians are rarely in a situation of epistemological experimentation, since by definition – except for those working on the present time, and in this case the frontier between disciplines perhaps doesn't mean very much – the object is always at a remove from them and their own interests as subjects are of a different order from that of direct involvement. So if we follow this line of argument, that might explain why, on the whole, the reflection of historians on their own practice is less sharp or less tragic than that of sociologists, and quite particularly that which you have undertaken in your books and interviews. The historical milieu perhaps serves in a good sense as a protection, since there is a lesser rift, but perhaps – I won't say in a bad sense – it produces a lesser lucidity in relation to the practice of knowledge. Thus the operation of these two opposite poles – one on the side of structures, the other on that of intentions – which divide types of sources, types of practices, and historians themselves, involves less of a rift, and makes it possible that at the end of the day very different approaches can coexist quite well in a field that is not completely unified but remains a kind of mosaic of research subjects and ways of doing history. So that you find the same tension that was our starting-point in this exchange, but with a lesser intensity.

PIERRE BOURDIEU: I'm very happy with everything that you've just been saying; it's a perfectly acceptable description of the difference between the historical field and the sociological field. I feel nostalgic sometimes for the world of history. I tell myself that I would be calmer if I were in this world, where you have *Les lundis de l'histoire*,[3] where you can have a discussion between the staunchest champions of economic history and the champions of the history of mentalities, and all is for the best in the best of all possible worlds. Besides, there are individuals who are quite ecumenical and serve as a bridge between the different positions...

ROGER CHARTIER: And besides, you give pleasure by writing. Particularly if you assign history the function – which it assumes voluntarily or fulfils by itself – of supplying roots, references, identities to those who perhaps feel a lack of these, both at the level of a community and at that of a national identity. In the end, the discussions we can have about sociology, which is held to be aggressive and enabling individuals to reappropriate themselves only at the price of much suffering, take place in a quite different order. Historical discourse, except in certain cases and for the history of the twentieth century, is a discourse that comforts and reassures.

PIERRE BOURDIEU: Everything that you've just said explains very well the different social treatment that historical writings and sociological writings receive. This is clear even at the level of bookshop sales; it

---

[3] See p. viii.

---

is hard to imagine offering sets of sociology books for Christmas presents, it would be quite unthinkable. I say this without being in the slightest degree aggressive; it is likely that, if I were a historian, I too would take part in the production of Christmas presents.

What I mean is that this raises questions about the difference between sociology and history. Sociologists are seen as aggressive people, conflictual, people who make a fuss [*à histoires*], whereas historians are people who don't make a fuss, as they work on things long past. From time to time, they start a new debate on the French Revolution...

What seems important to me is that you can say that history is a far more integrated discipline, more convivial, conforming more to the ideal of a 'scientific community'... If indeed this really is a community, which is actually a fiction. A scientific community is a site where people struggle for truth. And I believe that sociology, because it is conflictual, is more integrated. This is going completely against the grain of accepted ideas. People say: 'At least historians can talk among themselves; look at sociologists, they all tear one another to pieces, there aren't two who say the same thing, etc.' I believe that, contrary to what is commonly believed, it is only in the name of a completely archaic and simplistic philosophy of the scientific community that a privileged position can be given to history. And again it is in the name of one of these simplistic pairings that consensus and conflict are opposed. That is a fine subject for a dissertation: 'Do you think that society is based on consensus or conflict?' Who doesn't see that there is such a thing as a form of consensus through conflict? Firstly because, in order to argue, there must be a ground of agreement on the grounds of disagreement, and then because conflict leads to integration; integration is reached differently, not by compromise or evasion.

You said just now that each person has their little empire, their little fief, which makes for a comfortable life; medieval history never infringes on modern history. I think that one of the great weaknesses of history – all my friends are historians, I can't be suspected of any ill will – is that it is basically not subject to the kind of permanent test that the sociologist suffers, having constantly to justify his existence, and never being able to take this as given. To give a very concrete example, when I want to give out a questionnaire, I present myself as a historian. Whenever there is a difficult situation, I say to my students: 'Tell them that you're historians.' A historian has a right to exist, whereas a sociologist...

The fact, therefore, that sociology is a science '*à histoires*', which leads to problems, which creates problems, whose existence is in question, obliges it – at all events, a certain sociology – to a permanent lucidity about its own existence, an underlying anxiety that makes it basically more progressive scientifically.

ROGER CHARTIER: The tension that we have just been talking about can be given a historical dimension. What perhaps characterizes the specifically French case, in relation to other intellectual traditions, is that at the start of the twentieth century, with an intellectual strength that was not matched by the same institutional strength, Durkheim's project was able to present sociology as a kind of science of sciences, whose methods would unify all other disciplines. There are certainly in your scientific practice strong traces of this project, if only in the refusal to define sociology as working solely on the contemporary world. In this way, the convenient partition between historians who work on the past and sociologists in charge of the present is completely rejected. It is only necessary to open one of your books, or the *Actes de la recherche en sciences sociales*, to see that there are reflections or articles that bear on the nineteenth century or still earlier periods, which are traditionally the monopoly of historians. Do we not have here a trace of the very violent debates in the early twentieth century between the French sociological school, which was so strong, and the *Annales* around Marc Bloch and Lucien Febvre? What is the situation with the claim of sociology to be 'the' social science, able in any case to disturb historians and make them react?

PIERRE BOURDIEU: As far as I'm concerned, I have completely abandoned the ambition of a royal discipline that was so clearly constitutive of sociology. In the classification of sciences, as Auguste Comte presented this, sociology was at the summit, it was the crown. And I think that, in the rivalries between philosophers and sociologists, there is always the shadow cast by Comte, by his ambition. I think, for my part, that this is an ambition with no practical meaning. Another ambition, most clearly formulated by Durkheim, is equally strange to me, what you could call the Spinozist ambition to produce a truth that transcends particular interests. There is a very fine text of Durkheim's in *The Evolution of Educational Thought*;[4] you would think it was a translation of Spinoza's famous text on truth and error... You also find the same thing with economists. Samuelson begins his great textbook in the same way:[5] particular individuals have a partial and one-sided view of the world of economics; they are unable to totalize; these views are antagonistic, incompatible, not cumulative, whereas the scholar, for his part, has what Leibniz said about God – the sociologist does indeed often take himself for God – the geometric centre of all perspectives, the geometric convergence of all points of view. I believe that this was Durkheim's political ambition, you could even say a technocratic ambition: the sociologist with the knowledge of everything can tell particular individuals what is good for them, better than they can themselves; in other words, error is privation, error is mutilation, the fact of seeing only a little bit.

---

[4] Émile Durkheim, *The Evolution of Educational Thought* (London: Routledge, 2006).
[5] Paul Samuelson, *Economics: An Introductory Analysis* (New York: McGraw-Hill, 1948).

4
Habitus and Field

ROGER CHARTIER: I believe that one of the problems you are tackling, which is also a problem for historians, is what you have called the 'genesis of mental structures within biological individuals', that is, the process by which individuals internalize the structures of the social world and transform them into patterns of classification that guide their behaviour, conduct, choices and tastes. And it is with a view to understanding this incorporation of mental structures in biological individuals who have in common that they share the same social trajectory that you proposed an operational notion that is perhaps not traditional, at least in the recent state of the social sciences, and is that of 'habitus'. This notion may appear a little barbaric, or medieval. Why use it? And where does the concept come from? Did you invent it or adopt it? Or are you using it in order to oppose it to a different tradition – the older one of the history of mentalities, and in its early forms that of the *Annales*?

PIERRE BOURDIEU: The notion of 'habitus' is a very old notion, as it goes back to Aristotle, by way of Thomas Aquinas, etc. But I think that the genealogical perspective, which many people like to adopt today, because I reactivated this concept, does not bring anything to a concept. The scientific use of a concept presupposes a practical mastery, and if possible a theoretical one, of the former uses and the conceptual space in which the borrowed concept was used. And in fact one can draw a theoretical line based on this mastery of the space, which resembles the political line drawn on the basis of an intuition of the different political spaces through which structural constants maintain themselves.

The notion of habitus, as this is found in Aristotle or Aquinas, or subsequently in such different people as Husserl, Mauss, Durkheim or Weber, basically says something very important: social 'subjects' are not instantly formed minds. In other words, to understand what someone is doing, it is not enough to know the stimulus; there is, at a central level, a system of dispositions, that is to say, things that exist in a virtual state and then manifest themselves in connection with a situation. That's it, by and large. It is an extremely complicated debate, but the notion of habitus has several virtues. It is important for recalling that agents have a history and are the product of an individual history and an education associated with a milieu, and that they are also the product of a collective history, and that, in particular, their categories of thinking, categories of understanding, patterns of perception, systems of values, and so on, are the product of the incorporation of social structures.

Let me cite an example that is a little complicated but which, I believe, makes it possible to understand what I mean. I studied very recently the choices of students who, after their *baccalauréat*, have to orient themselves in what is today the extremely complicated space of the system of higher education.[1] You have to imagine this as a kind of forest: some go left, some go right, others get lost in byways and labyrinths... I studied how these people choose: why some are attracted by the École normale, others by the École polytechnique, the École nationale d'administration, etc. And I was led to say, on the basis of empirical data – on the basis of a study of the choices made, the characteristics of the people who made these choices, and the relation between the two – that it all happens as if the social agents, in this particular case the aspiring students, had internalized a structure of opposition that is the structure of objective opposition in the space they are entering, which is, by and large, the opposition between Haute école de commerce and École normale; on the one hand, business and the like, and on the other, intellectual things. Thus they possess systems of preference that are acquired in the family: you find more teachers' sons at the École normale and more shopkeepers' sons at the HEC. What is determinant in these choices? It is one of the major structuring oppositions of modern mentality: art/money, disinterestedness/interestedness, pure/impure, spirit/body, etc. It is this

---

[1] 'Agrégation et ségrégation: Le champ des Grandes écoles et le champ du pouvoir', *Actes de la recherche en sciences sociales*, 1987, no. 69, pp. 2–50 (with Monique de Saint-Martin).

quite fundamental opposition that comes to determine preferences in terms of cars, of newspapers read, holidays, relationships to the body, sexuality, and so on. This opposition, which exists in objectivity in the form of a distribution of practices, in the form of structures of distribution of products, etc., is internalized in the form of a system of preferences: faced with a choice between a position that is intellectually interesting but poorly paid, and a position that is very well rewarded economically but perceived as not intellectually interesting, if I am the son of a teacher I will choose the first of these. That is one example of how an objective structure – the opposition between the *grandes écoles*, which is an extremely complex system – becomes a subjective structure, a category of perception and appreciation, a system of preferences. By what mediation? Well, that's quite a job...

ROGER CHARTIER: This is where a discussion conducted from the historian's point of view can become pertinent. Working with the notion of habitus, there is an initial question that can be raised, that which Panofsky raised when he studied the homologies that existed, in the age of medieval scholasticism, between architectural forms and structures of thought: what is the site, the social matrix, that makes possible this inculcation of dispositions that are sufficiently stable and shared to function in very different fields of practices? Can we read what you have done as leaning in the direction of an incorporation of the two from the start? In some of your texts, particularly in *Le Sens pratique*, there is the idea that things are settled very early on, and that early childhood can be the key moment for the incorporation of social structure within individuals, even before the handling of language, even before the mastery of rational thought. Or do you rather believe that institutional mechanisms, for example the school, which you've devoted so much time and study to, subsequently add to, strengthen and correct what was an initial incorporation of gestures and behaviours by way of the unsaid? There is a major debate here, I believe, since the question is raised, on the one hand, of the relative importance of institutions, and on the other, of everything that is transmitted by seeing things done and by listening to what is said, which would thus be the very matrix of behaviours inculcated within the cell of the family, in the relation between parents and children.

PIERRE BOURDIEU: As a preliminary to answering this, I would like to take the opportunity to show the extent to which the individual/society opposition, on which a whole series of current debates is based (holism versus individualism, for example), is absurd. Society – to make 'society' the subject of a sentence is committing yourself to speaking nonsense, but I am forced to speak in this way in order to go quickly – society exists in two fashions. It exists in the objective world, in the form of social structures, social mechanisms, for example the mechanisms of recruitment to the *grandes écoles*, the mechanisms of the market, and so on. And it exists also in human brains, in individuals; society exists in the individual state, in the incorporated state; in other words, the socialized biological individual is part of the individualized social.

That said, this does not mean that the problem of the subject of actions does not arise: is the subject conscious or not? And here we come back to the problem you raise of the genesis of the individual, the social conditions for the acquisition of these fundamental structures of preferences: are things settled very early on? This is an extremely complicated problem. I think that there is a relative irreversibility, for a logical and quite simple reason: all external stimulations, all experiences, are perceived at every moment by way of categories that are already constructed. Thus there is a kind of closure. I believe, for example, that ageing can be defined as a kind of gradual closure of these structures. The person who ages is a person who precisely has increasingly rigid mental structures, ones that are therefore ever less elastic in relation to stimulations, solicitations, etc. This occurs very early on. The male/female opposition, for example. I will shortly be publishing a paper, which I heard in Chicago, by a psychologist who has done experimental work on learning about sexual difference.[2] It is quite extraordinary to see how, even before the age of three, boys and girls in nursery schools learn how to behave with someone of the opposite sex, and what one should expect to receive from a boy or a girl – blows or kindness respectively. These mechanisms are established very early in life. If you consider that the mechanisms of the sexual division of labour are very fundamental – in politics, for example, all political oppositions are sexual ones: submission/

---

[2] This is probably a reference to Judith Rollins, whose 'Entre femmes' was published in *Actes de la recherche en sciences sociales*, 1990, no. 84, pp. 63–77.

domination, on top/underneath, and so on – and if you consider that all the bodily patterns of perception of the division of labour between the sexes are very constitutive of the perception of the social world, you tend to believe that, to a certain extent, these first experiences are very strong. That said, the very great Russian psycho-sociologist Vygotsky – who was inspired by Piaget but introduced a socio-genetic dimension that for Piaget was something secondary – tried to analyse the specific effect of teaching at school.[3] He says some very exciting things. He starts from the example of language, which can be generalized: children arrive at school knowing their language, and yet they learn grammar. One of the major effects of the school is seen as the transition from practice to a meta-practice.

Habitus, therefore, is not a destiny; it is not a *fatum*, as people have me saying; it is a system of open mechanisms that can be constantly subjected to experience, and by the same token transformed by these experiences. That said, I shall immediately correct myself: there is a probability, which is inscribed in the social destiny associated with a certain social condition, that experience confirms habitus; in other words, that people will have experiences that conform to those that formed their habitus. I shall remove a further difficulty: habitus reveals itself only with reference to a situation; it is a system of virtuality. Contrary to what people have me say, it is in relationship to a certain situation that habitus produces something. It is like a spring, but it needs something to release

---

[3] Lev Vygotsky, *Thought and Language* [1933] (Cambridge, MA: MIT Press, 2012).

it. And according to the situation, habitus can do contrasting things.

I shall give an example right away, from my work on bishops; this is of great concern for historians. I had a longitudinal population. Bishops live to a very old age, and in synchrony I had side by side men of thirty-five and eighty-five years of age, thus people who had been constituted as bishops in completely different states of the religious field, who had become bishops in 1933, in 1936, in 1945 and in 1980. I had their social origin; I had sons of nobles, for example. And the sons of nobles who would have been bishops of Meaux in the 1930s, who would have had their parishioners kiss their ring, in the aristocratic tradition that Duby describes in his books, are today bishops of Saint-Denis, that is, they are radical, red, bishops. And in my view, if you understand properly what a habitus is, you will understand that the same aristocratic habitus of distance from the mediocre, the commonplace, the trivial, the petty bourgeois, can produce the opposite in opposite situations. In other words, it is the habitus that in a certain sense constitutes the situation, and it is the situation that constitutes the habitus. This is an extremely complex relationship: according to the habitus that I have, I either see or don't see certain things in a given situation. And depending on whether I see these things or not, I shall be incited by my habitus to do or not do certain things. This is an extremely complex relationship, which I believe none of our ordinary notions – subject, consciousness, etc. – enables us to conceive.

ROGER CHARTIER: And do you believe that this notion can have a possible use for the historian? In listening to you, I am struck by the affinities and differences with another of those authors who use the notion of habitus quite frequently: Norbert Elias, also a sociologist, and also a historian in a certain sense. Several historians, myself included, have tried to continue his reflections in order to try to understand how, in a very long-term process, the categories of mental life, but still more profoundly the whole psychological economy of individuals, came to be modified. With this question: is it possible to historicize the object that psychoanalysis designates? Do you believe this is a possible perspective? Such a perspective would introduce a notion of very long-run process, a notion with which you don't generally work, as your analyses are focused on the forms of habitus that generate patterns of appreciation, perception and action in the present of our societies. Does this mean that you reject as teleological, as too macroscopic, this kind of very long-run perspective that in a sense crushes the complexity out of reality? Or is it simply because the objects on which you work, even if they have a historical dimension, do not claim a long-run history since they are located by definition in fields constituted as such, that is, in social spaces that are unified at a given moment by stakes, oppositions and trajectories?

PIERRE BOURDIEU: This is a very difficult question. It is true that I have a kind of suspicion, a kind of methodical or methodological mistrust of the grand generalizations about tendencies that flourished in Marxism and post-Marxism, and that I believe are always a temptation for both historians and certain sociologists. One of the professional reflexes that I try to inculcate is mistrust towards comparisons of the before/after type: was it better in 1940 or 1945, more democratic or less democratic? That is a typical example regarding the education system. People fret over false problems of democratization, without seeing that we are dealing with two totally different structures, in which the rates of representation that are absolutized, of sons of workers, for example, do not have the same meaning at all.

For my part, I often preach distrust of these comparisons, and a fortiori of grand generalizations about tendencies: Weber's rationalization process, or the process of monopolization of physical violence by the state, of which Elias developed a certain aspect. Because I actually think that there is the danger of teleology, because there is also the tendency to transform the descriptive into the explanatory. I also have in mind Foucault's notion of 'enclosure'. Notions such as these make me quite uneasy.

Having said that, I will also say that out of all these problematics that of Elias is basically the one I find most sympathetic, because he does actually take as the basis of an evolving social-historical psychology a major real process, which is the constitution of a state that moves to monopolize first physical violence (I would add symbolic violence), then all forms of authority. The educational system, for example, is an enormous advance in the direction of the monopolization of the right to say who is intelligent and who is stupid. This process cannot but have effects on what I will call habitus, on what historians call, in a rather vague and dangerous word, mentality.

Now, more precisely, there is a further question, which is that of the social conditions of the constitution of controls. I think that a valuable study, a research programme – and here again, I believe that Elias sketches this wonderfully well, for the subject of sport[4] – would be to analyse, using indirect indicators such as sport, the prevalence of violence in a given society. I think that this would be a very good programme, on the understanding that violence would have to be studied in all its forms: physical violence, but also symbolic violence, insult. There are studies, like the one by Claverie and Lamaison, that are very interesting in this respect;[5] they show how, in peasant societies, a certain type of violence was always present, and that a number of mechanisms in these societies cannot be understood if one fails to grasp the importance of this symbolic and physical violence. The same holds for Kabylia: it is quite impossible to understand the whole culture of honour unless you know that these are societies in which an insult means that one risks one's life. For example, I believe that the life of intellectuals would be completely transformed if they risked their lives each time they insulted someone. Not to speak of symbolic murders...

ROGER CHARTIER: Perhaps we can stay for a moment with the example of sport, because I believe it allows us to understand what are the conditions of possibility, the transformations of habitus, that make possible a

---

[4] Norbert Elias, 'Sport et violence', *Actes de la recherche en sciences sociales*, December 1976, no. 6, pp. 2–21.
[5] Élisabeth Claverie and Pierre Lamaison, *L'Impossible mariage: Violence et parenté en Gévaudan* (Paris: Hachette, 1982).

---

confrontation without destruction, a collision without life being at stake. At the same time, this example allows us to locate very well the notion of 'field', which is the other fundamental concept in your work. You said, at the beginning, that the functioning of a habitus does not depend solely on its intrinsic nature; it depends on the place in which the habitus operates; and if the field is different, then the same habitus produces different effects. This notion of field, I believe, makes it possible to conceive discontinuity. You find again here the problem of nominalism, that is, that we need to have words, whether scientific or not, to denote institutions, objects, practices. These words may remain the same, but behind this stability they designate specific configurations. This can be demonstrated in politics, showing how there is always the political, but politics, as we understand it, historically refers to the constitution of a certain type of stake, a certain configuration of the public space. And the same is true for the case of sport. You can say that, from the Mayas through to today, there have been physical exercises involving the clash of bodies. And yet, what we can define as the space of sport today was born at a certain moment in time, undoubtedly in the late eighteenth century in England. This is where the problematics of historians and sociologists fuse completely, in the analysis of the conditions of emergence of these social spaces that are sufficiently unified for it to be possible to locate here the positions occupied by actors, their trajectories and their competitions.

PIERRE BOURDIEU: That's again a point where I both converge with Elias and diverge from him. I believe that Elias is more sensitive to continuity than I am. In the case of sport, for example, it seems to me dangerous to construct a continuous genealogy from the ancient Olympic games to the Olympics of today, as so many historians of sport do. There is an apparent continuity, but this masks a tremendous break in the nineteenth century, with the English boarding schools, with the educational system, with the constitution of a sporting space... In other words, modern soccer has nothing in common with ritual games such as *soule*.[6] It's a complete break. And the problem would be the same – and become even more astonishing – if we speak about artists. There is a temptation to say that Michelangelo and Julius II were like Pisarro and Gambetta. In actual fact, the discontinuities are tremendous, and there is a genesis of discontinuity. That's when it becomes interesting. In the case of sport, the discontinuity is quite sharp, in connection with the boarding schools, etc.

ROGER CHARTIER: At the turn from the eighteenth to the nineteenth century in England.

PIERRE BOURDIEU: Yes. Whereas for the artistic field we get the impression that this is a world that was taking its time to form. This begins in the Italian quattrocento, perhaps earlier; then gradually, as if by successive brush strokes, there is the invention of the artist's signature, then of the assessment of the work according to different criteria from the price of the painting...

---

[6] [An early kind of football, traditionally played between villages on festive occasions. – Translator.]

And you have to get almost to Manet, to the Impressionist revolution, for the artistic field to begin functioning as such; in other words, for a world to exist in which it is really possible to talk of such a thing as an artist. And I think that the same could be said of the field of literature; you could say, paradoxically, that before Flaubert writers were not artists. Here I am laying it on a bit thick, but this is to shock the historians: I believe that it is anachronistic to say that Michelangelo was an artist. Of course, historians are not naive and they do raise this problem; but they raise it in terms that to my mind are naive: at what moment was the transition from artisan to artist? In fact there was no transition from artisan to artist, there was a transition from a world in which you had people who produced according to the norms of economics, basically the norms of ordinary production, to an isolated world within the economic world which is an economic world turned upside down, in which people produce without a market, and where in order to produce you have to have enough capital to hold on, knowing that you won't sell a single product in your whole life; which was also the case with the majority of poets from Mallarmé on. This analysis needs a longer development, but when we project the concept of the artist or writer retrospectively onto periods before 1880, by and large, we commit fantastic barbarisms... And by the same token, we fail to see the problems of the genesis, not of an individual, but of a space in which this individual can exist as an artist.

Roger Chartier: Do you not believe that reading Elias forces both sociologist and historian to reflect on the role that we give to the forms of exercise of power and to the state in this gradual constitution of fields – a role that a certain history, whether social history or the history of mentalities, but perhaps also a certain sociology, attached to describing each of these fields separately from the overall social ensemble in which they are located, could have forgotten? It seems to me that this is where his work has a strong pertinence, by reminding us that these fields are always constituted in a relationship with the state, either because they are in themselves a kind of emanation (for example, in the case of 'artistic' practices in the age of patronage), or because, as in the nineteenth century, they constitute relatively independent spaces, located outside the sphere of the political.

PIERRE BOURDIEU: True. But that said, I would still diverge from Elias here, because I think he is a Weberian, and in fact the view that you are ascribing to him is actually that of Weber. This is in no way to diminish Elias's merits, because making a schema that was invented by a great scholar operate fully is already a tremendous scientific act, and if all scholars matched up to their scientific predecessors, science would be in a quite different state today, at least social science. That said, I think that you cannot find the true role of the state if you start with the state; for example, in the artistic field that I have tried to study, the Impressionist revolution was made both against the state – that is, against the Académie – and with the state. In other words, the problem of the state cannot be posed, it seems to me, until we know how fields function and, in particular, how worlds independent of the economic field are created. Then the state becomes the site of a meta-struggle, a struggle about power over the fields. This becomes very abstract, but I could argue in its favour: for example, citing the challenge of obtaining a law that changes the cost of housing or changes the age of retirement. What we have here is a trans-field struggle, but one that changes the balance of forces.

5
Manet, Flaubert and Michelet

ROGER CHARTIER: It seems to me that your work, in its most recent developments, has embarked on paths that were somewhat unexpected, particularly with your proposed study of Flaubert, Manet and the crystallization of the aesthetic, literary and pictorial field. Is this return to more elevated individuals and objects an effort to apologize for what is traditionally attributed to sociology, in particular what you have been doing: the boredom of quantification, the complexity of statistics, the interest in unimportant things? Does someone who has written a book on 'distinction', bringing in objects as undistinguished as the most ordinary foodstuffs and tastes, find here a way of relegitimizing their whole work by directing it towards more legitimate objects? Are you not in the process of subjecting yourself to a certain number of analyses that you have yourself proposed, by choosing a 'distinction' applying no longer to the work but rather to the objects?

PIERRE BOURDIEU: Some people will not fail to say that this is associated with ageing and social consecration… Which is in any case a general law for the evolution of scholars. Ageing is in no way a biological phenomenon. Consecration is very often accompanied by a change of objects: the more consecrated someone is in a field, the more they have a right to planetary ambitions. For example, scientists often have a second career as philosophers. With me, I have the feeling that this is not the case, and that it is the very logic of my work that has led me here. We could add Heidegger to the list that you gave. Another key thinker. Basically, Manet, Flaubert and Heidegger could respectively be considered, if you wanted to give awards, as the most painterly of painters, the most writerly of writers and the most philosophical of philosophers. So, why do I turn to study things like this? I think that what led me to them is the regular logic of my work, and particularly my research in understanding the process of genesis of a field. In the case of Flaubert and Manet, I see them as individuals who have to be viewed, basically, as founders of fields.

To take the example of Manet, which is clearest. There was academic painting, state painting; there were state painters, official painters who were to painting what philosophy professors are to philosophy – no offence meant – that is, people who had a career as painters, who were recruited by way of competitions, who had preparatory classes – the exact equivalent of the preparatory classes for the *grandes écoles* – with the same procedures of hazing, levelling, degradation and selection. And then an individual arrives: Manet. He went through the schools, which is extremely important. This is something that Weber says in passing in his book on ancient

Judaism;[1] there is a tendency to forget that the prophet emerges from the ranks of preachers; the great heresiarch is a prophet who says in the street what is normally said in the world of scholarship. Manet is like that: he is the pupil of Couture (a semi-academic painter), and he soon began to cause problems in Couture's workshop. He criticized the way in which models were made to sit, he criticized the antique-style poses, he criticized all this... Then he began to do something absolutely extraordinary: like a prize student who flunks the competitive exams for the École normale and goes on to challenge the École normale instead of internalizing its punishment as a sort of curse, something that we are very familiar with in the university milieu, he challenges the world of art and defies it on its own ground. This is the problem of the heresiarch, the head of the sect who confronts the church and opposes it with a new principle of legitimization: a new taste. The problem is to ask how this taste appears: what was there about Manet, his capital, his origin, his family, but above all his social world of connections, friends, etc.? I am doing work that, strangely enough, no historian has done, or else only in a purely anecdotal fashion. I am trying to study the world of Manet's friends, the world of the friends of Manet's wife – who was a pianist and played Schumann, which was avant-garde at that time – with a view to resolving a quite fundamental question: the person who leaps out of an institution, such as the university institution or other academic institutions, leaps into the void.

I mentioned the drama of the top student who fails his exams because many of our listeners have at least

---

[1] Max Weber, *Ancient Judaism* (New York: Free Press, 1967).

---

an indirect knowledge of this experience. The problem of such a person is that he cannot even think of challenging the institution that rejected him; this doesn't even come to his mind; and if he does think of doing so, he finds himself cast into nothingness. This was Manet's position: 'If I don't do academic painting, won't I just cease to exist?' People would say: 'He doesn't understand perspective!' How to prove that he does understand it, but deliberately refuses to respect it? To resolve all these problems – the solitude of the heresiarch, the fact that you need chutzpah to resist excommunication – you have to understand what Manet had in the way of those resources that are sometimes called psychological but which actually have social foundations: his friends, his artistic connections, and so on. That is the work I am doing. I am focusing on the most individual of individuals: on the particularity of Manet, his relationships with his parents, with his friends, the role of women among these acquaintances... And at the same time, I am studying the space in which he was situated in order to understand the beginning of modern art. Today people talk a lot about modernism. Previously, they asked what modern art was...

ROGER CHARTIER: Yes, but modern art is not the same thing as the establishment of a field of pictorial production. The overall constitution of the field, which also implies the positions of those who do not do modern art, necessarily refers to other determinations. Or do you think that the thunderclap that Manet represents was enough to recompose a whole set of positions in such a way that they cohabit as opposing positions within something that was new and is precisely the field of painting?

Pierre Bourdieu: You are completely right to correct me. I seemed to be giving a quite classic view of the solitary revolutionary, excluded, isolated, etc. This was quite wrong. I quite agree that Manet instituted a world in which no one could say any more who was a painter and what it was to paint properly. To employ a big word, an integrated social world, that which ruled in the Académie, was a world in which there was a *nomos*, that is, a fundamental law and a principle of division. The Greek word *nomos* comes from the verb *nemō*, which means to divide, to partition. One of the things that we acquire in the course of socialization is principles of division that are at the same time principles of vision: male/female, wet/dry, hot/cold, and so on. A well-integrated, academic, world says: 'This one is a painter, this one isn't a painter.' He is a painter because he is 'patented', because the state says that he is a painter, because he is certified as a painter – that was the Académie. From the time that Manet made his move, no one could say any more who was a painter. In other words, there was a transition from *nomos* to anomie, that is, to a world in which everyone can legitimately struggle over legitimacy. No one can say any more: 'I am a painter' without finding someone who will say: 'No, you're not a painter, and I can challenge your legitimacy in the name of my claim to legitimacy.'[2]

---

[2] 'L'institutionnalisation de l'anomie', *Les Cahiers du Musée d'Art moderne*, 1987, pp. 6–19 ['Manet and the Institutionalization of Anomie', in Bourdieu, *The Field of Cultural Production: Essays on Art and Literature*, pp. 238–53].

ROGER CHARTIER: Is this the definition of the field of modern art for you?

PIERRE BOURDIEU: Yes, it is. And the scientific field is of the same type: it is a world in which there is a question of legitimacy, but there is a struggle over this legitimacy. A sociologist can always be challenged in his identity as a sociologist. And the more the field advances and its specific capital accumulates, the more anyone wants to challenge the legitimacy of a painter, the more the challenger himself needs the specific capital of a painter. Take, for example, the forms of radical contestation used to challenge painting by today's conceptual painters, beginning with the slashing of canvases. Unlike narrow-minded iconoclasts, they need to have a tremendous knowledge of the history of painting in order to challenge painting adequately, pictorially. The specific iconoclasm conducted by an artist presupposes a virtuosic mastery of the artistic field. These are paradoxes, but they appear from the moment that there is a field. The naivety involved in saying 'He paints like my three-year-old son' is typical of someone who does not know what a field is. Another example is that of Le Douanier Rousseau, who was a naïf; but the naïf appears only when there is a field, just as the religious naïf appears only when there is a religious field. This is someone who becomes a 'painter for others', whom others see as a painter. It was people like Picasso and Apollinaire who made Rousseau a painter, by considering him from the painting field. But he himself did not know what he was doing. The opposite of Rousseau is Duchamp, who was basically the first to have grasped, in an almost perfect fashion

– which does not mean consciously – the laws of the artistic field, and the first to have played with all the resources that this institutionalization of anomie provides.

ROGER CHARTIER: But then, if we apply the same perspective to the constitution of the social sciences, would you say that the constituting of a discipline as a discipline is the equivalent of the constitution of a field such as you have just described it for the field of pictorial production?

PIERRE BOURDIEU: There has to be a game and a practical rule of the game. A field has a close resemblance to a game – many of the things that Huizinga says about games can be said about fields – but one of the main differences is that the field is a site where there is a fundamental law, rules, but not a *nomothete*[3] – not an authority such as a federation – as in sport – that lays down the rules. And finally, there are regularities immanent to the field, sanctions, censures, repression, rewards, without all these being instituted.

The artistic field, for example, has the particularity of being the least institutionalized of all fields. There are relatively few instances of consecration. You can certainly mention the Venice Biennale, but compared with the scientific field or the university field, the artistic field is relatively little institutionalized.

That said, if we take the example of philosophy, there is a field whenever someone wishing to enter the philosophical game with ideas that may be called 'Nazi' –

---

[3] Someone who sets the rules.

that was the case with Heidegger – is obliged to bend, without even proceeding by way of a conscious operation, to a set of laws of operation of this world: for example, 'being anti-Semitic' becomes 'being anti-Kantian'. In fact, there are mediations: Kant was defended by Jews as an expression of rationalism at the time that Heidegger appeared. What is interesting is this kind of alchemy that the field imposes. If I want to say Nazi things, but still be recognized as a philosopher, then I have to transfigure them, so that the question of knowing whether Heidegger was a Nazi or not is meaningless. He certainly was a Nazi, but what is interesting is to see how he said Nazi things in an ontological language.

ROGER CHARTIER: What you are proposing makes it possible to escape from the great reductionist naiveties. Historians, when they move from an analysis of social positions, social structures, to an analysis of cultural productions or practices, have practised as much as others, sometimes more than others, a kind of short circuit by directly relating production to position. Either at the level of the individual, very mechanically relating what is produced to the individual producer, or at the level of groups. Many discussions on the forms of 'popular culture' have got bogged down in this habit of setting up relationships without any mediation. And this is why I believe that the notion of 'translation', of 'mediation', of reformulation in a language and a system that is imposed by the state of the field, is a key contribution.

But I have the same question as with our discussion on the notion of habitus, a question pertaining to the '*longue durée*': what is the situation with the field before the field? How can we try to observe what may be said, at a given moment, in a language constituted and organized within a common space – even if the positions occupied there are completely contradictory and hostile – when this space does not yet exist? Let us take the case of the discourse on the social world that will become the particular object of 'sociology'. I am currently writing a study on Molière, which focuses particularly on *George Dandin*.[4] We can say that seventeenth-century theatre was one of the ways of examining social processes that would later be constituted in other idioms, other forms, in sociological knowledge. This does not mean going back to the idea of the precursor – the rather stupid idea of compiling a portrait gallery, and then, starting from Montesquieu or even earlier, saying, 'These are the ancestors of sociology.' This is a meaningless idea. On the other hand, seeking to understand what type of discourse makes it possible to focus on objects that would subsequently be constituted as the specific objects of a scientific field, that of sociology in the present case, does perhaps make sense.

PIERRE BOURDIEU: Certainly. Once again, you have just made a number of points. I could bring in another example, alongside that of Molière, that of the nineteenth-century novel. It is a commonplace to say that Balzac was the precursor of sociology. What is more, he saw himself as a sociologist and claimed to be one. For me, in fact, the inventor of sociology, the

---

[4] Chartier, 'George Dandin, ou le social en représentation'.

most sociologist of novelists, was Flaubert. This often comes as a surprise, as he was at the same time the inventor of the formal novel. And there was a whole effort, a wrong one in my view, on the part of the Nouveau Roman novelists and their critics, basing themselves on Flaubert's saying: 'What I would like to write is a book about nothing', to constitute Flaubert as the inventor of the pure novel, the formal novel, without an object, etc. In actual fact, Flaubert was the most realistic, sociologically, of all novelists, particularly in *A Sentimental Education*, and particularly because he is formal. You can say exactly the same about Manet, whose formal research was at the same time research on realism. And the antinomy between formalism and realism is another of those stupid antinomies. I believe that in Flaubert's case the work of formal research was the occasion of a social anamnesia, a return of the social repressed. As a result of purely formal research, a pure novel, a novel that did not consist simply in 'telling a story', Flaubert's achievement – which cost him a thousand deaths – consisted in 'spitting out' his own experience of the social world and creating an objectivation of the ruling class of his time that rivals the finest historical analyses.

When I did my first analysis of *A Sentimental Education*, I sent it to a number of friends, including a philosopher who asked me whether the view of the bourgeois social space that Flaubert offered was sociologically well founded. That raises a question. I believe that Flaubert was not completely aware himself that he was producing this analysis. This would raise the question of form, since it was by way of a work on form, which was at the same time a work on himself, a work of socio-analysis, that he produced the objective truth of what made him write a novel. It is naively said: 'Flaubert identifies with Frédéric'; is Flaubert Frédéric? Flaubert produced the novel of a character who occupied the same position as himself in the social space, and who, occupying this position, did not manage to write a novel. This could be extended indefinitely. I think that this raises all the problems of the functioning of sociology, the role of anamnesia, of socio-analysis, of the relation between the novel and scientific discourse.

One question caused me to reflect a good deal: why, when I present readers of Flaubert, lovers of Flaubert, with a translation into sociological language, in the form of a schema, of the content of *A Sentimental Education*, which they do not challenge for a moment, does this revolt them? Why does a novel that they accept as 'marvellous' – I think that *A Sentimental Education* is one of the novels that provokes most in the way of literary passion – repel them when it is retranslated into the flat, objectivizing form of scientific discourse? What is more, that experience is easy to test; I think that I would myself have been revolted, twenty years ago, by many of the analyses I am proposing today.

That said, it leads us to reflect on the forms of objectivation. I think that these forms vary according to the states of the fields involved. To use an analogy, at the risk of seeming complicated: wars of religion are the form that civil wars take in the state of differentiation of fields in which the political field is not yet differentiated from the religious field. At that point in time, there was a kind of inchoate struggle in which peasant wars were at the same time religious wars. It is foolish to ask whether they were political or religious: they were as political as possible within the limits of a space in which, since the political field is not constituted as such, the only terrain is religion. In the same way, I think that Molière, as you have shown in relation to *George Dandin*, can constitute a form of sociological objectivation: relations between bourgeoisie and nobility, struggles over systems of classification, etc. Flaubert says the maximum possible in the existing state of the systems of censorship and the specific censorship associated with the particular genre that is the novel, which is the most political genre.

ROGER CHARTIER: Yes, saying the maximum possible or saying it differently. We come back to a problem that we have already mentioned, that of writing. It seems, from everything you have said, that there is almost a nostalgic fascination in relation to literary writing, which perhaps speaks with an impact and force much greater than even that of the most accomplished, the most successful sociological writing, about the object that you have in mind. Perhaps this is a question to do with the state of the field: at a given moment, when sociological discourse is not constituted as such, literature – or perhaps other symbolic productions – occupies the whole terrain. It is both literary and in part sociological. From the moment when you come into a situation of competition, rivalry, dualism, sociology can be stigmatized as an inferior discourse, since it cannot render in the most legitimate language, which is that of literature, objects that are, however, common to both. We perhaps have an example here of the way in which the same discourse can change, not because it changes in itself, but because the field in which it is expressed has changed...

PIERRE BOURDIEU: Quite true, there is nothing I can add...

ROGER CHARTIER: But to return to literature as 'sociology', aren't there moments when you would like to be Flaubert?

PIERRE BOURDIEU: Yes and no. It is obvious that there is a certain nostalgia. That said, I think that the fact of being in a position to understand sociologically the reasons why Flaubert was Flaubert and why he could not be other than Flaubert (which is already extraordinary), the fact of understanding why he could not be the sociologist he wished to be (that is something we forget: he wanted to be at the same time the master of language, the master of form, and also – you only have to look at his work of documentation – he wanted to speak the truth about the social world), the fact of knowing this prevented him from dreaming of a discourse that would be in fact an alienated discourse. I think that to a certain extent the novelist Flaubert was unable to do completely what he wanted to do. He could only say what he said about the social world because he said it in such a way that it was not said, not admitted. Perhaps because he could only tolerate the truth of the social world if it was presented in a tolerable form, a proper form... People very often say to me: 'But in the end, you sociologists lag behind novelists.' I believe, for example, that Faulkner is a tremendous novelist of popular discourse. This may appear very surprising, but if I had to say where you find something like popular language – what you hear in interviews – I would say: in Faulkner. If novelists are often in advance, for example, in the understanding of temporal structures, in the understanding of structures of stories, in understanding the uses of language, and so on, this is in large part because, being occupied by the work of putting into acceptable form, they place reality at a distance; they touch reality with tweezers of form; and in this way they can tolerate it. Whereas the sociologist is intolerable because he says things just like that, without putting them *en forme*. The difference of form is both everything and nothing. It explains why the transformation that I perform when I make *A Sentimental Education* into a schema both changes nothing and changes everything. And it renders intolerable something that was charming because it was the product of a denial, and that was denied again by the receiver, who understands everything without understanding. Moreover, this has the charm of 'playing with fire', with the social fire that is something that no one wants to know.

ROGER CHARTIER: I believe that the relationship between modes of writing and scientific discipline varies according to the discipline involved. For history, it is easier to fit oneself, consciously or not, into forms of narration or recital borrowed far more readily from literary construction, as the issues at stake are not the same. In sociology, what is important is the distance in relation to the object itself. That's what makes the difference.

PIERRE BOURDIEU: Here I am often tempted to tease my historian friends. They have a concern with writing, with good form, that is quite legitimate, but often they spare themselves the raw vulgarities of the concept, which are extremely important for the progress of science. The concern for a good story can be very important because there is also a function of evocation, and one of the ways of constructing a scientific object is also to make it felt, make it seen, evoke it almost in the Michelet sense, though I do not care for this very much myself. Can you evoke a structure? That seems very strange, but it is one of the functions of the historian – as distinct from the sociologist, whose task it is, on the contrary, to disengage the immediate intuition: if he wants to explain an election night, he knows that the reader already knows too much about it; so he has to cut back, get down to the essential; while the historian, if he wants to talk about the Benedictine monks, can bring in the forest, etc. There is a function of fine style here. But sometimes, I believe, historians sacrifice too much to good form, and to that extent, do not carry through the break with initial experience, with aesthetic preferences, with the enjoyments associated with the object.

ROGER CHARTIER: Yes, and this is reinforced by the return to forms of understanding in which social actors fill the whole space, which brings with it the temptation for the historian to duplicate their lived experience. In this way he becomes responsible for the resurrection of dead souls, who find a new existence in his account. That is where the reference to Michelet is both powerful and necessary; but it can also be an obstacle for an undertaking that, in the way that yours does, seeks to articulate structures and individuals, position and habitus.